THE COVENANT SERIES:
WORKBOOK ONE FOR THE NEW COVENANT

God's Love

How Can We Experience It?
How Can We Offer This Love to Others?

"***A New Commandment*** *I give you you . . .*
As I have loved you, so you ***must*** *love one another.*"
Jesus (John 13:34)

Mark Johnson, MD

Carpenter's Son Publishing

God's Love: WORKBOOK ONE FOR THE NEW COVENANT

Published by Clovercroft Publishing, Franklin, Tennessee

Published in association with Larry Carpenter of Christian Book Services, LLC
www.christianbookservices.com

Edited by Bob Irvin

Cover and Interior Layout Design by Suzanne Lawing

Printed in the United States of America

ISBN: 978-1-968127-12-1 (print)

ABOUT THIS WORKBOOK SERIES

This three-volume Workbook Series is designed to accompany *The New Covenant*, volume three of *The Covenant Series* by this author.

God extends an offer to each of us: a New Covenant relationship with Himself. He designed this relationship to display His love toward us and require our love in return. In Scripture God speaks of lives that are *radically transformed* within this relationship. We are a "new creation." God intends that we live very different lives going forward. But is this always the case? Instead, do many people's "new lives" bear far too much resemblance to their "old" ones?

Why is this? If we search the Scriptures for guidance, we mostly end up with a list of rules—the *dos and don'ts.* Often we do not understand exactly *what* we are to do—when, for instance, we are told to "love others as God loves them." Often we do not understand *why* God tells us to do certain things, or why we should want to do them. Often, even if we sincerely want to follow God, we do not understand *how these things* would be possible for us—when, for instance, we are told to emulate the life of Christ in our daily lives. Where do we look for answers to these *what, why,* and *how* questions?

Fortunately, there are answers to these vital questions. These answers are found within Scripture, but to fully understand what God means when He instructs us to, say, "put off our old life and put on our new one," we must understand something else. To understand these words, and many other things God says about our old life, our new life, and the path from one to the other, we must understand *the nature of our Covenant relationship with God.*

Everything God instructs us to do in Scripture flows directly from the *structure, nature, function,* and *purpose* of this relationship. Few people are aware of these answers, though, because few people in our Christian culture—including pastors and seminary teachers—correctly understand this relationship. To do so, one must go back to the time of Jesus' life on earth, to the original understanding of Covenant.

The New Covenant sets forth this historically correct understanding. As we carefully examine this relationship, we see something else: God's plan *within this relationship* to accomplish everything He intends for our lives.

Within Covenant, God has *already provided everything necessary* for us:

1.) **The total transformation of our true self,** deep within the core of our being.

2.) **The plan**—by which the rest of our self is transformed. God intends that we develop a *pure heart*, so our deepest desires become *the things of God.*

3.) **Every resource needed** for the dramatic life change God desires.

Within Covenant, we literally become an extension of God's life. He expects us to conduct ourselves accordingly. Why is God's desire not fulfilled in many lives?

There is one more variable in play here in addition to God's will. That variable is us. God's plan assigns to us many tasks and responsibilities. But we must choose to carry out His plan. Every Christian faces a vital question:

"Will I embrace God's plan, and make the most of my one-and-only life?"

Even if we understand Covenant, see God's plan, and want to follow His plan in a general sense, this in no way ensures that *God's desire will become our life.* This outcome requires the strongest possible commitment on our part. We must choose to become *unremittingly faithful* to God and His plan. We will only make this kind of commitment if we are thoroughly convinced that God's plan is our best possible choice.

To make the most of God's offer we must understand a few more things. This additional understanding is the focus of this Workbook Series.

1.) **The Goal of God's Plan**: what He intends our "new life" to be.

2.) **God's Plan and Our Faithfulness**: what God requires from us within Covenant, and why we should want to do what God instructs us to do.

3.) **The Journey Toward Christlikeness**: what will we experience on this journey? How can we overcome the external and internal challenges we will face?

VOLUME ONE: *GOD'S LOVE*

We need to see more clearly the life God desires for us. What would this life *look like* and *feel like*? What benefits would this life provide versus any other choice? We need to understand why *we may not desire* elements of this life. Then we can determine whether our resistance is based on truth and reality or upon a several-millennia-long campaign of deception by God's enemy. This enemy's efforts are designed to *keep us from living our best life.* We will only devote ourselves to God's plan if we desire the life God offers to us more than any other.

VOLUME TWO: *GOD'S PLAN / OUR FAITHFULNESS*

To build any complex thing—a house, or our new life in Christ—*we need a step-by-step plan.* We must first build a proper foundation. Then we build each element, in a certain order and a certain way. If this is done well, we end up with a beautiful, high-quality house—or our best life. Done poorly, or with no plan at all, what happens next? God provides the plan and every needed resource within Covenant to build a new, radically transformed, vastly better life for everyone who is in Covenant with Him. This is without question.

"Why do you call me, 'Lord, Lord,' but do not do what I say? As for everyone who comes to Me and hears My words and puts them into practice, I will show you what they are like. They are like a man building a house, who dug down deep and laid the foundation on rock. When a flood came, the torrent came and struck that house, but could not shake it, because it was well built. But the one who hears my words and does not put them into practice is like a man who build a house on the ground without a foundation. The moment the torrent struck that house, it collapsed and its destruction was complete."

LUKE 6:46-49

The variable in God's process of life-transformation is us. Dismantling one life and building another requires the full commitment of our mind, heart, and will. If Jesus is truly our Lord, we will make this commitment and back it with our life. But we will only choose to engage in this lifelong, challenging process if we actually make Jesus our Lord versus simply saying that He is.

VOLUME THREE: *THE JOURNEY / WHAT WE WILL EXPERIENCE ON THE PATH TOWARD OUR BEST LIFE*

Despite all that we may know, want, or intend—and despite all that God has done and provided—living out God's plan on a daily basis is challenging. Walking this path hand in hand with God requires all that we have—and far more. This is the most exciting, rewarding, gratifying, and beneficial journey we will ever make. But we must overcome a series of external and internal challenges if we are to do, be, and become what God desires.

Based on more than forty years of my own journey, and walking beside many other people on their journeys, this Workbook Series offers insight and guidance that can help us savor every delight and overcome every obstacle.

FOREWORD

WHAT ARE WE *REALLY* SEARCHING FOR?

Many today feel apprehension, both in the Christian community and the world in general. The world is concerned about the latest crisis that threatens to push humanity over the edge into oblivion—just as crises have threatened to do throughout human history.

The reason for apprehension is different among Christians. As evil forces grow palpably stronger in our nation and around the world, our standard, comfortable version of Christianity does not match up well with the challenges we face.

Our young are moving away from Christianity in record numbers, often toward things that God's Word describes as "evil." For young and old who profess to be Christians, large percentages engage in behaviors that fall into this same category.

What happens when a generation discards prior concepts—God's concepts—of what is right and what is wrong? We have epidemics of mental illness, fear, criminal activity, mass shootings of children by children, and confusion … about fundamental realities like one's gender. Beneath it all is a generation's lack of understanding of how to build a good and satisfying life—coupled with anger that no one taught them how to do so.

Regardless of where we stand on any issue, two things unite us. First, we all seek answers to extremely serious and threatening problems. Second, the lives we want, and the world we want, would be characterized by *love*. Yet the search for love in our world is a frustrating journey down wrong roads, while the search for love among Christians involves gestures and slogans more than substance. Nearly all, it seems, have trouble finding enough love in this world—from others, or within ourselves.

At some point we need to consider what love is in the first place. *How does it come to be*—first, within us? Then, *how can love grow among us*? When we consider these things, what answers do we discover? What plan emerges? What is needed, and what resources are available? Or are we just pursuing a foolish, romantic fantasy?

Love. The word flows through our minds and hearts … through songs, literature, and slogans. *"What the world needs now … " … "all we need is …" … "put a little love in your heart, a little heart in your love…"* True love is perhaps the consummate human experience, both in giving and receiving. But what is true love, and where is it found?

If we are honest, love is one of the most needed elements of life. If we disagree, we have simply given up—and concluded that love is not possible for us. The search for love motivates vast human effort. But love can be elusive … fickle … fleeting … futile … betrayed. We yearn to receive it more than we have learned to offer it. We know what it *could be* in the depths of our soul, but we settle for what we can get. We have made peace with the reality of our world—that true love is rare. We grapple with its lack—from those who are supposed to love us, and those who say they do. We grapple with its opposite: indifference, contempt, disdain, hatred … and the impact of these things within us. We hear of God's love, but experiencing His love is another question.

God, who created our hearts, knows precisely what we need. He issued His most important instructions to His followers near the end of His life on earth. They were charged with the responsibility of meeting the deepest need of those around them—by loving each other as God Himself loves them (John 13:34). Then, in His final words to His followers before departing this earth, Jesus told those present to teach His future followers "to obey all that I commanded you" (Matthew 28:20). These were Jesus' two primary themes. His followers were to love and obey.

As we will see, these two are one and the same. We cannot have one without the other.

THE ANSWER TO OUR BIGGEST QUESTIONS AND DEEPEST NEEDS

Perhaps the biggest issue is that we do not recognize, understand, or appreciate *the answer that is right before our eyes.* This book series has several obvious themes. But it would be easy to miss the one that is perhaps most important of all.

PERCEPTION VS. REALITY: A VITAL INSIGHT ABOUT HOW WE LIVE

Have you watched two equally capable people deal with basically the same situation, yet handle these situations completely differently? One overcomes the challenge. The other fails painfully. Going forward, these lives head in totally different directions. One person continues to be successful. The other life is characterized by defeat, depression, dysfunction, and discontent. What is happening here?

The greatest variable in life outcomes is *not the reality* of our circumstances or our resources. The greatest variable is *what we believe about these things.* One person *believes* he or she has the necessary resources to succeed. He or she therefore plans to succeed, then takes the required steps. He or she is willing to work as hard as necessary to develop and use these needed resources, then adjust and adapt along the way as needed to get the job done.

These same resources are available to the second person. But instead of recognizing and acting upon this reality, this person's course is determined by … what? By what he or she believes is true: that the necessary resources are *lacking*, that he or she *can't*, or *shouldn't*; that the problem is *simply impossible to overcome*. Or they just don't want to make the effort. This second life is directed in unfortunate ways by wrong beliefs … even though all that was needed to build their best life was freely available.

God lays an offer before us: a new, radically transformed, much better life. Scripture describes this life in terms of specific beliefs, attitudes, values, and actions. This life also turns away from a set of opposing beliefs, attitudes, values, and actions. God ultimately directs us to choose the most constructive behavior in any situation.

The centerpiece of God's offer is to *re-create us and restore us to a proper relationship with Himself* so we become able to build an intimate, loving relationship with our Creator. From our *transformation*, and *unique bond* with God, flow all the other changes—the radically transformed life that God desires, a life which leads to radically transformed relationships. Our changed life is first about receiving God's love, and then it is about learning how to give and receive actual love instead of our culture's cheap substitutes.

What is God's plan for your life and mine? Most today say it is to enter a relationship with Him and secure our eternity. But once in this relationship, what else are we supposed to be doing? Show up, listen, smile, and say nice things to each other? How does this get us to a radically transformed life? Experience suggests that it does not.

I bear witness that God's plan for our lives impacts every fiber of our being and every moment of our lives. After living out this plan for forty-seven years, and walking beside many others in mentoring relationships, I can say with confidence that anyone who follows this path will find a life that is abundant beyond their wildest expectation *on this earth*, much less in the life to come. But to build such a life we must follow God's plan. And to follow this plan, we must first discover it. This book series is about God's plan.

My dear children, for whom I am again in the pains of childbirth until Christ is formed in you, how I wish I could be with you now and change my tone, because I am perplexed about you!
GALATIANS 5:19, 20

God's plan is the perfect product of a perfect Being. He understands our minds and hearts as only their Creator could. His plan is highly effective if followed. What is the intended endpoint of His plan? We are to become *accurate reflections of the life of God* while on earth so we can carry out our assigned roles and build His Kingdom.

God's plan has proven effective in countless thousands of lives for two millennia, yet this is not the outcome for many of those who profess to be Christians. Why? Because God's plan to produce these outcomes, though evident in Scripture, is rarely taught or followed. God is clear about the consequences of following Him, or not following—on this earth and in eternity. It would be a tragedy of epic proportions for any believer in Christ to let slip through his or her fingers the remarkable, miraculous offer God extends to us … and not make the most of their one and only opportunity.

Until we all … become mature, attaining the whole measure of the fullness of Christ.
EPHESIANS 4:13

God offers us a restored relationship, and the opportunity to be like Him in every way that our finiteness allows—if we actually follow Him and do what He says. His offer is real and His plan works, but we must carry out His plan. To accomplish His desired outcomes, we must devote every fiber of our being and every moment of our lives to Him and His plan. In fact, His life must become our life, while every other consideration fades into the background. Welcome to God's Covenant plan for our life.

Contents

PRELIMINARY QUESTIONS

TRUE OR FALSE

God intends the life of every Christian to be radically transformed versus our "old life"	T ______ F ______
Life transformation is solely a gift from God; we play no part in this process	T ______ F ______
True love is a *heart issue,* not a choice	T ______ F ______
Living our new life versus our old life is a choice God calls us to make	T ______ F ______
"Loving as God loves" is possible for any Christian	T ______ F ______
Every Christian achieves God's goals for his or her life	T ______ F ______

What is God's ultimate goal for your life?

____

____

Why are some Christian lives more transformed than others?

____

____

What is the relationship between obedience and love?

____

____

What prevents us from loving, and how can we overcome this obstacle? Or can we?

____

____

CHAPTER ONE

AN IMPOSSIBLE COMMAND?

"A new command I give you: Love one another.' As I have loved you, so you must love one another."
JESUS, QUOTED IN JOHN 13:34

As we read Scripture, we put the things God says into categories. In one category are things we understand and agree to do. In another we put things we don't understand, disagree with, or don't want to do. Into a third category we place things we are told to do or be that seem impossible for us. And, at this moment, they probably are.

As we grow in understanding and maturity in Christ, though, we often find these seemingly impossible things to now be possible. Forgiving someone who grievously wronged us, for example. But no matter how mature we become, and no matter how well we understand Jesus' teachings, **everyone stops in their tracks as they read Jesus' New Command. Why?**

The more we understand the depth, breadth, and consistency of God's love, the more we simply stare at these words. The more we understand how *different* God is from us—He is perfect in every way, versus our lengthy list of imperfections—the more we simply stare at these words. **God can't be serious, after all. But is He?**

Teachers try amusing devices to downscale this command into something that is—in our minds—doable: *"Be nicer, a little more kind, more sacrificial, less selfish."* Seriously, is cherry-picking a few aspects of God's love an adequate response to God's command? At the same time, I suppose we would all agree that this command seems to be impossible for us mortals. How should we respond to His words?

DOES GOD ACTUALLY EXPECT US TO DO WHAT HE SAYS?

We need to carefully consider the words God uses. Jesus does not phrase the above statement as a general principle, or an instruction, or a suggestion. His wording draws listeners back to the other Commandments that were the centerpiece of Jewish morality and worship of God—all ten of them. Now Jesus, speaking as God, offers an eleventh Commandment. Does He intend that we take His words seriously?

Fear God and keep His commandments, for this is the duty of all humanity. For God will bring every deed into judgment, including every hidden thing, whether it is good of evil.

ECCLESIASTES 12:13, 14

Of course, we are taught that in the New Covenant we are "not under The Law" (all of the legal and ceremonial practices God conveyed through Moses) but "under grace." Many take this to mean that, as Christians, we are simply to recognize that we are imperfect. We are to be grateful to a merciful, gracious, and forgiving God for "saving us" from the consequences of our wrong choices. Then we go to Heaven. End of story. **In this way of thinking, our life as a Christian is not at all about keeping the rules.**

Therefore, when God tells us in Scripture to choose "X," but we continue to choose "Y," the real answer to the discrepancy between the way God says to live and the way we choose to live is the grace, mercy, and forgiveness of God. If this is true, God must hold no realistic expectation that our lives will come into alignment with His directives. Nor should we expect this from ourselves. We are simply content to be "saved" from a miserable eternity.

Are we free to *not follow* Jesus' New Commandment and His other directives? Or is being *under the law of grace* in reality a much more challenging assignment? **Are we now charged to love others instead of following a stack of rules?** Love is about more than *what we do*. Love is also about how we feel, our attitude, our sense of connection, and many other things—all of which certainly translate into actions. But we can also *do right things for wrong reasons* (see the Pharisees for details). Under the law of grace, God wants more than rule-following! But at no point are we free from His rules—which confine us to the most constructive choices for ourselves and others.

"Teacher, of all the Commandments, which is most important?" "The most important one," answered Jesus, "is … <u>love the Lord your God</u> with all your heart and with all your soul and with all your mind and with all your strength."

MARK 12:28-30 (EMPHASIS IS MINE)

"Whoever has my commands and keeps them is the one who loves me."
JOHN 14:21 (EMPHASIS IS MINE)

"Therefore go and make disciples of all nations, baptizing them in the name of the Father and the Son and the Holy Spirit, and teaching them to obey everything I have commanded you."
MATTHEW 28:19, 20 (EMPHASIS IS MINE)

According to Jesus, our most important duty as a Christian is to love God. He equates obeying God with loving Him. In His parting words, Jesus instructs His disciples to teach future followers to obey all that He commanded them to do. What of this suggests that He views obedience to God's rules as irrelevant? So how comfortable should we be if our lives are out of sync with His commands in any way, much less in the most important aspect of our relationship with Him: our love for Him?

That, however, is not the way of life you learned when you heard about Christ.
EPHESIANS 4:20

Jesus characterizes carrying out His commands as something *we can be and should be taught to do.* Our initial response to His New Command may be: "Impossible!" Can this directive be carried out in any situation? *Can we learn to do as He says?* Who is going to teach us to love, and how? The obvious answer is: "God"—through His Word, input from His Spirit, and from lessons drawn from our relationship with Him.

What have you been taught about what God does in our relationship with Him?

____

____

____

What were you taught about what we are to do in our relationship with God?

____

____

____

When you hear the term "obedience to God," what comes to mind?

____

____

____

LOVE LESSONS FROM SCRIPTURE

God's instructions about love in Scripture are a progression. We are first told to love ... essentially everyone, including our enemies. But most verses do not further define love. Love can mean many different things. To be more precise, God next tells us to "love others *as we love ourselves*" (Galatians 5:14, emphasis mine). This is an altogether different thing. Throughout life we have displayed single-minded devotion to bettering ourselves and our lives. Redirecting this same effort toward everyone would surely make our world a better place, if we would—or could—figure out how to follow this instruction.

On the other hand, how good a job do we do, really, of finding the path of greatest benefit for ourselves? Are we not at times misled, mistaken, shortsighted, and remarkably irresponsible? Some are more gifted at self-destruction than others. But all of us need to be protected from ourselves at times, even if we have the best of intentions. With this in mind, God ups the game. Rather than simply directing our sometimes misguided sense of love at others, He instructs us to love our brothers and sisters in Christ *as He loves us* (John 13:34).

Where do we start if we want to follow God's command? We start *where we are, with what we know—or think we know.* Then we move forward, willing to learn and change.

Consider what someone will do and be toward us if they truly love us. He or she will be warm, kind, committed, devoted, loyal, faithful, honest, and many other things. He or she will strive to do what is best for us in the long term. He or she will celebrate our victories, share our burdens, and mourn our losses. There is a special connection, a bond between us that is difficult to describe but easy to feel and see.

There are warm feelings and affections—emotions which seem to drive many of the loving actions. But something deeper than feelings is involved. There is a willingness to sacrifice, if necessary, for our well-being. He or she will always be willing to provide for our needs, protect us, and defend us. Beyond this, even if we harm or wound that person, there is a commitment to us that makes this relationship remarkably resilient. If we all related to each other in these ways, it would certainly build better relationships and better lives. So why don't we consistently relate to others in these ways?

Answer: because we have many other priorities. Even on our best days, loving others is only one of those priorities. Even if we are overwhelmed with love for another person, there are always thoughts, feelings, and agendas within us that drive us to be unloving. Of course, we all know that our unloving attitudes and behaviors have a lot to do with other people's imperfections. "If they would just ..."

Then we consider our love for God—One who is perfect in every way and loves us perfectly. He created us, and everything we enjoy, in life. Then He brought us into an eternal relationship with Himself. He has done more for us than we can possibly imagine. All He asks in return is that we love Him with all of our heart, mind, soul, and strength. Are we there yet? If not, why not? Is at least part of the problem, then, *our ability to love?*

At this point, what do you think would be needed for you to love like God loves?

____

____

____

WHO IS RESPONSIBLE FOR OUR ABILITY TO LOVE?

We are often told, "God does it all." This statement is strictly true when it comes to *our entry into His Kingdom*. The offer of *a new life in a proper relationship with God* is engineered totally by God. But this notion is often extended to include the entirety of our Christian life. This thinking assigns full responsibility to God for any significant change *within us*—thus also for the *lack of change* if we are struggling with things we need to change, or things God says should be different. Life-change is often thought to be a "God thing," not an "us thing." This obviously includes our capacity to love. Is this teaching true? Who is ultimately responsible for our lack of love: us or God?

When we are out of sync with God, aren't we "just being ourselves"? "God loves us just as we are," we are told. He loves us no more or less based on our actions (which is strictly true). So, do God's commands even matter? If they do, how can we possibly determine to make the changes God calls for—first *within ourselves*, then *in all the ways we relate to God and others*? This all coalesces into a key question:

How can *who we are* change?

Fortunately, God has a plan to produce what He commands.

What is your experience with life-change as a Christian? How did this occur?

____

____

____

WHAT IS LOVE FROM GOD'S PERSPECTIVE?

Before we consider God's plan, we need to better understand what He is instructing us to do. Let us return to our central question: "What is love from God's perspective?"

In the Old Testament, a single Hebrew word encompasses every aspect of God's love for us: ***hesed***. This word includes *what goes on within a person*—thoughts, beliefs, feelings, values, etc.—and the beneficial, merciful, and compassionate actions that *flow from one's inner life.* God's perfect inner life translates into perfect love.

Also, significantly, *hesed* refers to God's perfect faithfulness to His Covenant with us. If we are to love like God, is faithfulness to our Covenant with Him on the to-do list? If faithfulness to God's plan within Covenant is the path to revising our inner life, to bring it into alignment with God's perfect life, does His plan require *our faithfulness* to succeed? Yes, it does.

In the New Testament, God's love is also termed **agape**. Though frequently used, this word is not further defined beyond noting that it means "God's love." If we commit ourselves to *agape* someone, or to imitate God's *hesed*, where do we start?

Are we nicer, more kind, more sacrificial? Do we stop trying to get our way in situations, and instead support the often-equally-selfish agenda of others? Do our real needs exist only to be ignored as we devote ourselves to meeting the needs of others? Do we accept, or at least tolerate, everyone—and celebrate everything they do? All of these are held out as love in current Christian teaching. **Do these ideas accurately represent the heart of God's love?**

Scripture describes love in certain ways and as certain things. These descriptions certainly help. To love first means to "do no harm" (Romans 13:10). In 1 Corinthians chapter 13 love is characterized by fifteen brief descriptions. (These are very much worth studying.) These and other Scriptures offer important general guidance. In a given situation, however, what most closely aligns with God's love? What would the most loving intentions look like if lived out? Does love include things that go beyond our best intentions? How can we know what is *truly beneficial* in a situation in the short and long term, for ourselves and others?

At this moment, what do you think God means by: "Love others as I have loved you"?

____

____

____

GOD'S PLAN IS FOUND WITHIN THE RELATIONSHIP HE DESIGNED

Fortunately, these questions have answers. The answers are found *within* the God-designed Covenant relationships we enter with Him, or with our husband or wife. God created the New Covenant to display His love toward us, and to require our love in return. God created the Covenant of Marriage to build love-for-a-lifetime relationships, meet our deepest need for human intimacy, build loving families, and secure the future of coming generations. To answer our questions about love, we must understand these two relationships and God's instructions for conducting them.

This book series is not a theological discussion. Our journey toward loving as God loves—toward *living out God's plan to become like Christ*—**is practical and personal.** We must understand God's plan and what it requires. We must commit to His plan, then back up this commitment with myriad daily decisions over the course of our lives.

In my forty-plus-year Christian journey, the information set forth here about the *nature of a Covenant relationship* is the most important thing I have learned. Covenant explains everything we are to do or be as a Christian. Covenant explains what must occur to enter a relationship with God, and what occurs within us and between us as we do so. Everything we are called to do, be, think, feel, and celebrate in our Christian life flows directly from the realities, nature, structure, function, and purpose of our Covenant with God. **His entire plan for our lives literally resides within this relationship.**

If everything God tells us to do is in Scripture, **what is added by understanding this relationship?** Covenant explains everything that God instructs us to do in Scripture, then adds *two vital elements.* In Scripture, we are presented with an assortment of things to do and be. We find these in direct commands, stories, lists, parables, and object lessons. In short, *this information is there.* But when we read Scripture, at best we end up with a list: do this, and not that; be that, and not this. But why?

"'Because I say so,' says God" is a sufficient reason in a general sense. But wouldn't it help to know more about *why*? For many instructions (like *"love Me with every fiber of your being"*), wouldn't it help us to know *how*? How can we become able to do as we are instructed? Covenant provides not only the *what*, but also the *why* and the *how* for everything God tells us to do or be—including *loving as He loves.*

God's instructions in Scripture are like close-up photos of parts of a landscape. This list of dos and don'ts are like a stack of these photos. What we see is true and real. What is missing is the *context.* We do not know how all of the things we see relate to each other, fit together, and work together. Covenant provides a panoramic view, the "big picture" of how each element relates to all the others to form a huge, interlocking, incredibly beautiful puzzle that is intended to become the picture of our lives.

Welcome to God's Covenant plan for your life and mine. Happy reading!

PRELIMINARY QUESTIONS

In what ways have you loved other people?

In what areas do you want to be loved more, or better?

In what areas do you struggle to love?

What is the relationship between God's love and our love?

What three elements of God's love are described by *hesed*?

How can each of these elements be enlarged or improved within ourselves?

Do you believe our capacity to love can grow? How?

How would you describe the Covenant relationship we have entered with God?

CHAPTER TWO

COVENANT

HOW WELL DO WE UNDERSTAND THIS RELATIONSHIP?

God designed the Covenant of Marriage and the New Covenant to address the deepest needs of the human race. Many who read this are in one or both of these relationships. However, it is possible to be *in* a relationship and yet *not fully understand* the nature, purpose, or principles of the relationship. What does it mean to be in a Covenant relationship?

WHAT A COVENANT IS *NOT*: 'A CONTRACT, BUT ONE WRITTEN BY GOD'

Few people today, including Christian teachers, seem to understand the fundamental nature of this relationship—or its purpose, or the potential God placed within this relationship. Most currently teach that a Covenant is "a contract, but one written by God." This is entirely incorrect. A contract *commits us to certain behaviors*. We are rewarded for compliance and punished for noncompliance. We obey the stipulations of a contract purely because we choose to do so … or not. This concept of a relationship with God is the foundation for *legalism*: "It's all about following the rules."

A COVENANT CHANGES WHO WE ARE

A Covenant, in sharp contrast, *changes who we are*. Two are joined together, not by a set of agreed rules for behavior, but by *an exchange of life* between the two. This exchange *blends the lives—the very essence of each being—together within both beings*. This exchange therefore *alters the identity* of each being in the process. This co-mingling of two lives joins the two in the most intimate possible bond.

Thus, the two no longer have separate lives. Instead, they share a conjoined life. Scripture terms this condition "one," or "one flesh."

The model for this relationship is also the author of the relationship: *the Trinity.* These three distinct beings *share an identity*, and are literally *within each other.* Each is fully God; together, they are fully God. Scripture explicitly links the relationship between the Trinity with our relationship to God, and to each other within the Body of Christ (John 17:20-23).

Every other part of God's plan for these relationships—each principle and practice—is a logical consequence of the changes that occur *within* us and *between* us when we enter the relationship. **We do what we do because of *who we have become.*** This understanding is the only sufficient motivation to follow God's plan for these relationships. If we are a Christian—yet we are not firmly on track following God's plan for our lives—it is most likely because we are not properly motivated to do so … because we do not properly understand the relationship we entered with Him.

Every Christian has heard the terms and concepts we will discuss in this series. If we are a Christian, we are told we have undergone a new birth and are a new creature. We have heard that the Holy Spirit lives within us, and we are now "in Christ." But do we understand what these words mean? How many understand these realities—to the point that we base our beliefs, viewpoints, and lives upon them? Instead, are these simply *ideas*—things we say we believe? Ideas that have no connection with how we perceive ourselves, or our day-to-day life, or how we perceive God, or our relationship with Him? If so, our lives are far less impacted by this relationship than they could be, or should be.

"Traditional" marriage maintains some vestiges of the historic understanding and practices of Covenant. But once we see the entirety of God's plan for Covenant and how to fully develop this relationship—and fully develop ourselves in the process—we see how little our culture understands about these relationships, even within the Christian community. This explains why many Christian marriages struggle, or perish.

THE HISTORIC UNDERSTANDING OF COVENANT RELATIONSHIPS

I was introduced to the historic understanding of Covenant in Kay Arthur's Precept Bible Study, *Covenant*, in 1983. As Mrs. Arthur described this relationship, at several points she referenced a book by H. Clay Trumbull (*The Blood Covenant: An Ancient Rite and Its Bearing on Scripture;* 1885). I was able to obtain a copy of his book. For me, the understanding of Covenant that Trumbull set forth, after a massive amount of study and research, has done more to inform and direct my Christian life and marriage than any resource except the Bible (with which his work completely correlates). This historic understanding is notably different from what we are currently taught about this relationship—if this vitally important topic is mentioned at all.

Why is this information so important? In Scripture we are told to be different from what we now are in many ways. God's instructions for life-transformation within Scripture—though brief—become clear once we properly understand this relationship. But, if we do not understand the changes that have *already occurred within us, or the changes that still need to occur within us, or God's plan by which those changes occur,* **we will not understand the Scriptural instructions.**

Thus, current teaching glosses over and misconstrues God's plan by simply saying "God does it all." But He doesn't. He does *all of some things*. In other scenarios, God assigns the responsibility for life-change to us. God will not pour His choicest blessings into the lives of those who *do not carry out their assigned responsibilities*. We can be, and should be, taught to obey Christ in these ways. But are we?

What, specifically, is required from us within Covenant? The three highest priorities within Covenant are: 1) unremitting faithfulness to the relationship and to our Covenant partner; 2) consistent love-in-action toward our partner; and 3) honoring our partner above all others, and this relationship above other priorities.

Historically, the New Covenant and Marriage are recognized to include duties, obligations, and responsibilities that align with these priorities. **These are all logical results of the changes that occurred within us and between us. These also align with God's instructions in Scripture**, which is no surprise because God is the Author of both the Scriptures and this relationship.

To build the best relationship with God, the best marriage, and the best relationship with our brothers and sisters in Christ, we must play our God-assigned roles in these relationships and fulfill these responsibilities.

THE REALITIES OF A COVENANT RELATIONSHIP

Or do you not know that he who is joined to a prostitute becomes one body with her?
For it is written, "The two will become one flesh."
I CORINTHIANS 6:16

But the one who is joined to the Lord becomes one spirit with Him.
I CORINTHIANS 6:17

THE FUNDAMENTAL REALITY OF COVENANT

Within these relationships, God first causes a fundamental change to occur *within* each party, as the identity/nature/life of each enters the other, and remains there. The other 's life has now been received into the core of one's being, and vice-versa. The *identity of each party is now altered* to include the life of the other. This creates a unique bond of *shared identity*—the foundation upon which everything else in this relationship is built.

God then lays before us a plan to *become and build* everything else needed to accomplish His purposes within Covenant. He provides every needed resource. This is the reality. However, what we actually build within this relationship is guided by our *understanding*—not necessarily by God's provision or intent. Thus, *we need to bring our understanding into alignment with these realities and God's plan* for best results.

The fundamental reality of Covenant is to become "one flesh" in marriage (Matthew 19:5-6), or "one spirit" or "one" with God (Romans 8:9) in the New Covenant.

For the life of the flesh is in the blood …
LEVITICUS 17:11

AN EXCHANGE OF SOMETHING CONTAINING ONE'S LIFE

It was widely believed in the ancient world that the *life*, or the nature/spirit/identity of a person—the part that makes me *me*—resides in the person's blood. This is also God's view as stated in Leviticus 17:11 (above). A second body fluid was also (correctly) understood to represent one's life: the male's semen. For from it, plus a woman's egg, a new person is created. This outcome of sexual intercourse is obvious to all. What is less obvious—as noted in I Corinthians 6:16—is that sexual intercourse also joins two people in a "one flesh" bond (regardless of their intent).

In Matthew 19:6, Jesus notes that this joining is "what God has joined together" (not what biology has joined together). He follows this with "… let no one separate." A physical exchange initiates this relationship. But the insertion/alteration of our identities and *the joining that results between the two* are solely acts of God.

A wedding ceremony does not initiate the Covenant of Marriage. Instead, this joining is accomplished later in the most intimate possible way—if the couple has reserved their first intercourse for this moment, in keeping with God's Word. If not, the actual joining has already occurred (I Corinthians 6:16). Then why have a wedding? This ceremony acknowledges that marriage is a divine gift. It allows the couple to make vows to each other and before God in keeping with the historic duties, obligations, and responsibilities of marriage. And this joining can be celebrated with family and friends.

In the same way, husbands ought to love their wives as their own bodies.
He who loves his wife loves himself.
Ephesians 5:28

Once this exchange/joining occurs, the identity of my wife lives within me and mine within her. *Our lives become, in a literal sense, an extension of the life of the other*—a reality often illustrated by changing or sharing one's name. God tells us to "love the other as we love ourselves." He now makes this easy, for **what we do for our spouse we are literally also doing for ourselves.**

AN EXCHANGE OF BLOOD ALSO CREATES A COVENANT

A Blood Covenant is entered in an analogous manner through an exchange of blood between the parties (such as the Covenant between David and Jonathan, which David terms "a covenant of the Lord"—I Samuel 20:8). Blood Covenants were a part of life in ancient Israel and throughout the ancient world. Thus, the writers of Scripture did not exhaustively spell out the realities of Covenant; instead, they assumed this understanding in their readers. Unfortunately, there is no such "community understanding" in our current culture, a reality that has created much confusion.

"Very truly I say to you, unless you eat the flesh of the Son of Man and drink His blood, you have no life in you … Whoever eats my flesh and drinks my blood remains in Me, and I in them."
John 6:53, 56

But as many as received Him, to them He gave the right to become children of God,
even to those who believe in His name.
John 1:12 (NASB)

WHAT EXCHANGE INITIATES THE NEW COVENANT?

To enter a Covenant, we give our lives to each other, then devote our lives to each other. The New Covenant is entered with a God who is not bound by time and space as we are. Jesus provided a key part of this transaction more than two thousand years ago. When we accept His offer of relationship, He provides the remainder of the exchange. Much is written about "the blood of Jesus shed for us," almost always in terms of His sacrifice and His payment for our sins. These aspects are certainly real and true. **But there is another element in this picture that is often not recognized.**

Jesus' death paid *the penalty of death* for our sins (Galatians 1:4). His shed blood certainly (and correctly) evokes an image of animal sacrifice within the Old Covenant (I Peter 1:19; Revelation 1:5). But God offered more than forgiveness through His outpoured blood as He hung on the cross. ***He also extended***

to us an offer to partake of His life. Go back and read John 6:53, 56 (above) in this light, and see if these verses make more sense.

We have only to ***believe in*** **Him and** ***receive*** **His life** (as well as forgiveness for our sins and His Lordship over our lives), ***and then give Him our life in return.*** But there is one more element: ***our new birth.*** When we give our life to Jesus, He immediately puts our "old life" to death. Then, we are raised to a new life as a new creation, now in a state of oneness with Him. We must keep an important question in mind: "Why do we need this new birth / new identity / new life?" (John 3:7, 2 Corinthians 5:17, Galatians 6:15) Why are we not simply forgiven?

We celebrate what is commonly called the "Lord's Supper" to remember something (Luke 22:19)—but what? **We celebrate the point in time when the life of God—His Spirit—came to reside within us** (Romans 8:9-11) **and we came to reside within Christ.** To do so, we take a symbolic representation of Jesus' blood/life into ourselves in the form of wine or grape juice. By physically bringing this representation within ourselves we recall what God has done, and what we are called to do as a result.

The term "in Christ" (Ephesians 2:6) is not a metaphor. This describes our current reality in a New Covenant relationship with Him. Our life/identity came into Him (Colossians 1:27), and His life/essence/identity/Spirit came into us (Romans 8:9). *We therefore become, in a literal sense,* ***an extension of the life of God****, and vice versa.*

In what ways do these realities alter our view of our Covenant relationship, or our view of our Covenant partner, or the way we conduct a Covenant relationship?

If a husband and wife are now an extension of each other's lives, instead of two separate individuals who agree to be together, would this reasonably change the way the two approach their life together? How?

____

____

____

If we have now become a literal extension of the life of God, instead of just someone who "has a relationship" with God, would this reasonably change our approach to living? How?

____

____

____

ARE WE ALWAYS AWARE OF THESE CHANGES WITHIN AND BETWEEN US?

If everyone who enters a Covenant with God, or is married, has undergone the changes just described, **why aren't these concepts obvious based on our experience?**

We need to be aware of an important concept: **the difference between what we perceive and what is real. Something may be real**—and significantly impact us—yet we remain unaware of it. Early workers with radiation were unaware of the peril to which they exposed themselves. Many died before a connection was made between, say, licking a paintbrush between each stroke as a worker painted radium onto watch dials, and the variety of cancers these people developed. In a similar way, the changes God works within and between us offer us vast new opportunities and benefits—yet we may be partly or wholly unaware of of these important realities.

God contrasts walking by faith with walking by sight (II Corinthians 5:7). What is the difference? **God reveals things to us that we cannot perceive.** He shows us spiritual realities behind things we can perceive, but misunderstand. We must choose between trusting our perceptions (walking by sight) or trusting God's words (walking by faith).

What role has God's revelation (Scripture) played in your life in the last month?

____

____

____

If we are not guided by God's revelation, what does guide our life?

____

____

____

Many things occur in the depths of our being. Some we perceive clearly, some partially, and some not at all. **None of us can look within ourselves and see the fullness of our identity.** This resides in the core of our being, overlaid with many other parts of us. None of us can answer the question "Who am I?" fully and completely at any point in time. We spend our lives trying to get at the answer through our experiences. Why? So we can live "an authentic life," a life that reflects *who we really are.* We somehow know that this is the only life truly worth living. **But who are we now, within Covenant?**

We need *the God of all truth* to teach us about our world, Himself, and—especially in this case—about ourselves. We can only learn from Him about things within us and between us that are beyond the reach of our perception. **Though beyond our sight, these changes have massive potential to change the course of our lives.** But this potential may remain unnoticed and thus undeveloped. Once we understand these changes, we can understand God's plan for our lives. We begin to see these changes in operation—within ourselves and all around us. The life that each of us builds will be determined by *our understanding*. How important is it that we have a *correct* understanding?

What is your experience with walking "by faith" versus walking "by sight"?

____

____

____

What realities has God revealed to you that you could not perceive on your own?

____

____

____

THE PRINCIPLES AND PRACTICES OF A COVENANT

Let us first outline the logical consequences that flow from the exchange of natures and the joining that creates a Covenant. All of these items reflect the teaching of Scripture. If one is well-versed in Scripture, specific references will come to mind for each item. If not, the reader is invited to correlate these principles with God's Word.

IF ANOTHER LIFE NOW RESIDES IN THE CORE OF OUR BEING ...

— Each being becomes an expression of the life of both parties.

— There is no more "my life" and "your life." These have literally ceased to exist. Instead, there is only "our life."

  * This applies not only to one's sense of identity, but to *all aspects of life*.

  * *Our life* is to be shared in every respect. There is no "personal space."

  * At the same time, we *do not become the other* ... I do not become female by marrying my wife, nor do I become God by entering the New Covenant. I am simply joined to my wife or God by a unique bond of shared identity. His Spirit does live within the core of my being.

— Each now assumes the same responsibility to care for the life of the other that one has to care for oneself.

— From this global responsibility flow the duties, obligations, and responsibilities that have historically accompanied this relationship.

  * These involve *offering resources, attention, and effort as needed.*

  * These specifically include *provision, protection, and defense of the other*—at whatever price is necessary, including the cost of one's life.

— The interests of the other *are now as important to us as our own interests.*

  * We are responsible for promoting, protecting, and ensuring their best interests.

  * We are responsible to offer any needed aid in this pursuit.

— The "things of life" are freely shared as needed, or held in common. We assume *joint responsibility for family relations, friends, enemies, assets, debts, etc.*

— The correct answer within Covenant to the other's request is: "*Whatever I have, whatever I am, can do, or can become is at your disposal.*"

  * However, this does not mean an immediate "yes" to every request any more than Jesus answers "yes" to every prayer request.

  * Instead, our responsibility is to do *what is truly best for the other* at every point. This is the definition of true love.

— The other is to be *honored, above and before* all others.

— Since the other now occupies the core of our being, *they, and our relationship with them, become our highest priorities.* All other considerations are now secondary.

GOD'S DEFINITION OF LOVE

If we consider all of the above principles and practices of Covenant, **these are in sum an excellent functional definition of "love-in-action."** In fact, ***this is God's definition of love.*** God created Covenant to display His love toward us, and to require our love in return. Each item in the above list involves a large portion of our lives. In sum, no area of life is left untouched by a Covenant relationship.

Let's take a closer look at some of the above points, and see how these translate into daily life.

Can you see how the fundamental realities of Covenant lead to these principles and practices? What are your thoughts about this connection?

Which of these realities, principles, and practices do you already understand, and which are new to you? Are you surprised by any of them?

How is life impacted by realizing that "my life" no longer exists, only "our life"?

How is life impacted by the mutual responsibility to care for the life of the other?

How can we care for God's life?

Does understanding Covenant offer more clarity about God's instructions in Scripture? How?

How do you react to the Covenant principles regarding possessions, involvement in others' lives, the relative importance of others' interests, and the overall priority of our Covenant obligations?

COVENANT RELATIONSHIPS ARE ABOUT CONSISTENT LOVE-IN-ACTION

Covenant relationships are about giving and receiving love, learning how to love, and increasing our capacity to give and receive love. **Imagine being married to someone who approached your relationship in the ways outlined above.** Would you feel loved? Would you *be loved* in every way that matters? Imagine how your spouse would respond to someone who approached marriage in this way.

God's Covenant plan is the path to the best relationship, to building love-for-a-lifetime relationships. But to do so, we must recognize several other aspects of this relationship.

— **God designed Covenant as an "all in" kind of thing.** This relationship requires consistent and unremitting commitment, devotion, focus, and effort.

— **Covenant is a mutual thing. Both parties are to be "all in."** There is no "giver/taker" distinction (unless one party is disabled). Instead, there is to be a reciprocal giving and receiving.

— **The totality of these requirements is beyond the reach of any of us at the outset.** Ongoing personal growth and transformation are needed to fulfill our responsibilities. Our commitment to become *increasingly faithful* drives us to make these additional, necessary changes. These changes in turn produce maturity in Christ, or in our marriage. **Covenant is God's plan to grow both relationships and people.**

Our priorities dictate the life we will build. How does God change our priorities within Covenant? How would these changes impact our life and relationship?

____

____

____

Can we already spot a mismatch here? Between what we are used to doing, want to do, know how to do, and can do ... versus what God wants us to do? How are we supposed to handle this discrepancy? Does God have a plan for this?

____

____

____

____

____

GOD HAS ALSO OBLIGATED HIMSELF TO US IN THESE WAYS

God approaches His relationship with us according to these same principles and specifics. We are in Covenant with Him, and He is in Covenant with us. He is more aware of the principles of Covenant than we are, and has already obligated Himself to be all of these things toward us. One aspect of *hesed*, the Hebrew word for God's love, is *His faithfulness to His Covenant with His people.* We can count on Him to be perfectly faithful, and to always act in our best interests (though from our vantage point this truth may not always be evident; we may define "our best interest" differently).

Have circumstances ever caused you to question God's love for you, or toward someone you love? How did you handle your questions? Does an understanding of Covenant offer any help in such situations?

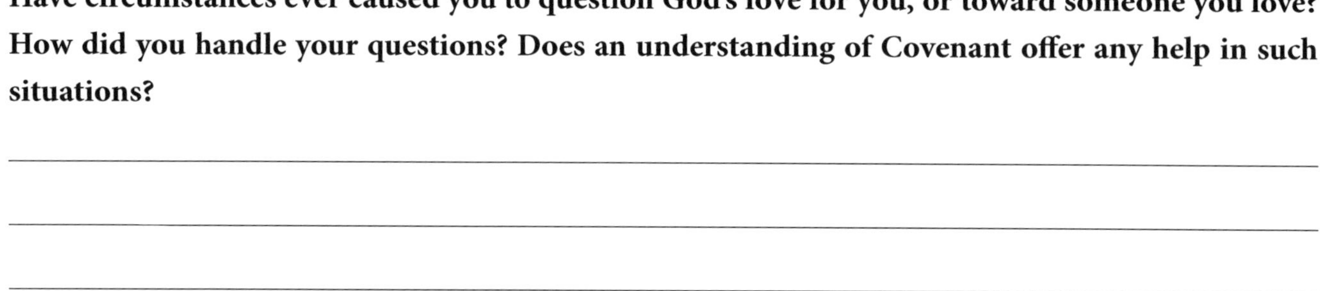

So we, who are many, are one body in Christ, and individually members one of another.
ROMANS 12:5 (NASB)

" ... that all of them may be one, Father, just as You are in Me, and I am in You."
JOHN 17:21

OUR RELATIONSHIP WITH THOSE IN THE BODY OF CHRIST

Let us consider one more aspect of Covenant. The definition of being in Covenant with someone is ... what? That our identity "shares space" with the identity of someone else, be that with another human or God. Now, if the identity of *every believer* resides together within Christ, and if each of us has the Holy Spirit/Christ/God within us, what is our relationship with others in the Body of Christ? Are we also in a Covenant relationship with every Christian? If this is true, are the realities and requirements of this relationship fully in place? Does this explain the ways Jesus and God's Word tell us to treat our brothers and sisters in Christ?

Now we must consider what it means to be in a marriage, and/or the New Covenant with God, and with our brothers and sisters in Christ.

Consider for a moment all the implications of this reality. While we reduce God's command to love our brothers and sisters to a few sound bites, God instead expands His command. *We are to love our brothers and sisters in a way that involves every aspect of our self and life, and every aspect of everyone else's self and life.*

It would be helpful to pause a moment and return to the above outline of the Principles and Practices of a Covenant. If you are married, go down this list with a view toward your relationship with your husband or wife. If you are a Christian, first go down this list in light of your relationship with God, then for your relationship with your spouse. Then do so for your relationship with each of your brothers and sisters in Christ. Consider the practical implications of each item.

Record your thoughts.

CHAPTER THREE

OUR CORE QUESTION: THE DEFINITION OF GOD'S LOVE

THIS DEFINITION MUST ALWAYS ARISE FROM SCRIPTURE

Let's return to the reason we are engaging in this discussion in the first place. *We are trying to define God's love so we can display His kind of love toward others.* We just considered a lengthy list of the things we are to do and be within Covenant according to the historic understanding and practices of this relationship.

Obviously, if we are trying to know the heart of God, our ultimate understanding cannot be based on cultural practices, but only on His Word. **We must cross-check these elements of principle and practice with His Word.** I have spent forty years doing this, especially during the process of writing a several-volume set of books on Covenant. H. Clay Trumbull, whose research and writings provided the foundation of understanding upon which this book series is based, did the same. He was a highly respected Christian teacher, author, and editor in the last half of the 1800s. I encourage you to search out these principles and practices within Scripture for yourself.

We love, because He first loved us.

I John 4:19

OPENING OUR EYES: GOD'S COMMITMENT TO US AND HIS LOVE FOR US

Everything expected from us within Covenant corresponds to God's commitment to us within this relationship. How has God loved us in these ways? We may be deeply loved—but we may not recognize, understand, or appreciate this love.

However, the more we recognize, understand, and appreciate God's love, **the more we will experience His love in the depths of our being.** The more we have this experience, the better equipped we will be to love others in similar ways, and the more motivated we will be to do so—**for we understand their benefit.**

In what ways has God loved you? List some here.

____

____

____

PRAYING IN FAITH

When praying for our own needs or the needs of others, we want to pray *in faith*—confident that we are praying according to God's will. If we pray that God will act *in line with His Covenant obligation to us,* we know that we are praying according to His will. These obligations were noted in the previous chapter.

Of course, the way God chooses to provide what we need may be different from how and when we think He "should" answer. Our hearts should always be grateful for His perfect responses—***whether we find them to be perfect in our eyes or not.*** Do these situations offer us an important opportunity? If our agenda differs from God's, can we now learn something about *what is truly in our best interest, or the best interest of others* in His eyes? Even Jesus learned obedience through the things He suffered (Luke 22:42, Hebrews 5:8); after doing so, He received blessings from the Father in response to His obedience (Philippians 2:6-11).

HOW DOES OUR LOVE COMPARE WITH GOD'S DEFINITION OF LOVE?

Refer again to the realities of Covenant and God's definition of love-in-action within Covenant in the previous chapter. Let us compile these into a checklist that we can use to assess our approach to others. If our love is out-of-sync with reality, or with God's approach, what can we do about this?

DOES WHAT WE THINK, BELIEVE, VALUE, SAY, OR DO ...

1) Reflect our connection with God, and accurately reflect His character and holiness?

2) Reflect our responsibility to support the interests of God—to build His Kingdom?

3) Honor God by totally trusting His Word, and totally entrusting our lives to His care?

4) Display our loyalty and devotion to God and to those in His Body?

5) Reflect our responsibility to love God through our faithfulness and obedience?

6) Reflect our connection with those in His Body? We are an extension of each other. Therefore, we fully accept each other and support each other's interests.

7) Reflect the reality of our family relationship with God and our brothers and sisters?

8) Fully share in each other's lives—burdens, trials, sorrows, joys, and victories? Is there space in our life for others, and do we make them a proper priority?

9) Reflect our willingness to share material support, time, effort, and attention as needed? And our willingness to protect, defend, and provide for each other?

10) Reflect our responsibility to become more mature, faithful, and loving?

11) Deal with others in redemptive ways, helping them to become more honorable?

12) Reflect the true priority of my interests versus the interests of others—as neither more or less important? Reflect the realty that God understands my needs and the needs of others far more than I do? Therefore, His priorities, agenda, and directions must always rule.

13) Recognize that "my" resources are a stewardship from God, to be deployed as He directs—toward my needs or in the direction of others? Also, to always keep in mind that the resources available are not just what we can see, but God's inexhaustible supply? Therefore, if God directs, we may be sure He will provide.

14) Recognize the priority of my Covenant partners—God, as my most important relationship and priority? Next, my spouse, and those in the Body of Christ? These are the highest priorities in my life. Every other consideration, priority, desire, and agenda is of less importance.

15) Reflect the ways we would want to be treated in a similar situation?

16) Recognize the importance of a request for help from a brother or sister in Christ, in light of the "correct answer" within Covenant to such requests? We should always be open to the possibility that a response of action, prayer, or resources may be our responsibility before God.

A word of caution here: openness to help does not ensure an automatic "yes" to every request. Our own needs are also important—no more so than other's needs, but no less either. Our control of our life and its resources is a "stewardship"—delegated authority from God to shepherd and care for what is ultimately His (Acts 5:4, I Corinthians 4:2). God entrusts resources to us to be used for our benefit, or for the benefit of others. These resources may be God's answer to another's needs, but we do not say "yes" to every request because God may have other plans.

We are always to ask Him how He wants His resources to be used, then do so. He wants us to develop good judgment and wisdom in these matters and to bring our priorities and values in line with His ***so that His life is formed within us.***

MAKING OUR PERSONAL CHECKLIST

The above checklist is only a beginning point. I recommend that you formulate your own list and use it. We should enlarge it over time as needed. The above list is what *we should do*. But I have also found it helpful to voice this list in the negative: "Am I about to say something that will dishonor, be disloyal, etc.?" ***Our personal list should reflect what to do, as well as what not to do.***

THREE PRACTICAL EXAMPLES

Consider the vast impact these Covenant principles can have in everyday life if we live them out. *These realities and principles are total game-changers*—and this is the point. Grasping and implementing these realities will produce a radically different way of life versus our old life under the guidance of our culture. Let us look at three examples.

THE "COMPETING KINGDOMS" MODEL VS. THE COVENANT MODEL

According to "the world" (whose ideas ultimately come from the prince of this world, Satan), our best life is found by *"my life, made better."* And how is my life made better? The real win, according to this view, is getting *my way*—if necessary at the expense of others. Thus, two married people view themselves as having a separate Kingdom and Queendom. These separate kingdoms are continually contending for scarce resources. The key is to *get my way* as much as possible. What happens next?

A pattern of attacking and undercutting each other emerges. Why? Each tries to improve his or her negotiating posture by weakening the other party, in an attempt to get *my way* more often. Such relationships are filled with competing agendas and manipulation, along with whatever pleasantries brought these people together in the first place—if any still remain. *Getting my way to enhance my life is the preferred endpoint, regardless of the damage inflicted on the other party or the relationship.*

Good-natured people may still manage to build decent relationships upon this foundation. But this mindset is also the foundation for a lifetime of contention, unhappiness, frustration, abuse, and failed relationships.

How does Covenant change this picture? Within Covenant, two people (should) approach each other entirely differently. **First, "my life" no longer exists. All energy is directed toward building "our life."** The agenda, needs, and desires of each person are equally important—and each is equally charged with meeting the legitimate needs of both. Thus, these two must get to know each other in order to learn each other's needs, desires, likes, dislikes, hopes, and dreams. **Each then embraces the other's considerations as their own.**

When ideas and agendas conflict, the path is not to *be right,* but to *get it right,* on balance, for both parties. The needs of both are discussed in a supportive environment, and may need to be clarified. When my wife and I consider each other's reasoning, we often find ourselves switching sides, arguing for the other's position!

But frequently an even better thing happens. As we work through reasons and options, **we often come to a solution that neither of us saw at the outset—one that best meets both of our needs.** Everything about these scenarios builds the relationship. After all, isn't this the point?

There is no "I win, you lose" within Covenant. If you win, I win. If you lose, I also lose—and the relationship loses. If I think making *my life* better at someone else's expense is a win, I merely pay an unacceptable price to build an illusion. *My life* no longer exists.

People will pay good money to watch two determined opponents contend on a football field or tennis court. No one would pay to watch someone sit in a chair and mutilate themselves. That would be deranged. *But that is precisely what many couples do—mutilate themselves as they attack each other*, and all in the name of … what?

God's intent through Covenant is to build love-for-a-lifetime relationships. How does the above approach to our interests impact our hearts for each other?

____

____

____

How does this approach improve decision-making?

____

____

____

ACCEPTING OTHERS … WHILE NOT ENDORSING THE ENEMY'S PLAN

All of us have a wall in our lives. On the inside of this wall are all the people we view as "us"—people we identify with, our family, people we understand, people whose lives are headed in the same direction, people with similar beliefs, etc. These are the people who matter. These are people we notice, focus on, reach out toward, and build things with. We feel a sense of kinship with them. They are our friends and allies.

Then, there are those outside our wall. These people are different. We do not share key elements—beliefs, values, ethnic background, and more. These people are *them,* not *us.* We do not notice, try to understand, reach out toward, or want to build anything with these people. They are misled, inscrutable, perhaps dangerous. They are obstacles, and perhaps enemies. *We turn our backs to them.* In our minds and hearts *we reject these people.*

Before we think this is just about racial, ethnic, national, or religious differences, consider how often we put people who have become "the problem" outside our wall. This might be an annoying neighbor or coworker. Or the teenager down the street. Or the teenager down the hall in our own home … or a parent … or our spouse. Whoever they may be, people outside our wall are no longer worthy of our notice or effort.

Covenant does not *abolish* our wall. It does, however, change the way we determine who is within our wall, and how we regard those outside our wall. Consider these three scenarios:

The first scenario involves someone in a Covenant with us—a spouse, or a brother or sister in Christ. This person may be annoying, weak, immature, dishonest, a troublemaker, misled, or simply wrong. He or she may have wronged us. He or she may have crossed a line morally or ethically, or may have violated common sense or our sensibilities. While it may be right to step back, assess, and take corrective action, *we are never free to withdraw our acceptance from this person and turn our back to them.* Why is this so?

The issue of full acceptance is already settled. Our spouse has already been fully accepted within us. We can pretend things are otherwise, but we are merely pretending. The same is true of our brothers and sisters in Christ. **When we accepted Jesus within us, these folks came along within Him as a package deal.**

Consider all that we signed up for within Covenant—to devote ourselves to bettering the life/lives of our Covenant partner(s). *That someone acts like an idiot, or worse, does not impact our responsibility within Covenant.* Nor does some difference between us in belief or practice. Instead, these illustrate the importance of our mutual responsibility to help each other become more like Christ—through prayer and constructive engagement when appropriate. Scripture illustrates many of the principles and practices needed to play this redemptive role in each other's lives.

In sum, we are to invite people *who are already within us* to follow the same path to life we are following—the one detailed in Scripture and outlined in this workbook series.

How might the reality that "we have already accepted another within ourselves" impact the way we view difficult situations and difficult people?

___

___

___

What principles and practices within Covenant, and within Scripture, offer guidance to deal with these challenges?

___

___

___

For our struggle is not against flesh and blood, but against the rulers, against the authorities, against the powers of this dark world and against the spiritual forces of evil in the heavenly realms.
EPHESIANS 6:12

The next scenario involves someone who is outside of God's Kingdom. This includes any lost person who is acting like a lost person—as lost people will do. These people may be vastly more different from us in ways that feel more threatening to us.

These people are genuinely on the other side of a wall from us—the wall that divides God's Kingdom from the kingdom of darkness. Yet we are still to regard and treat these people in particular ways. While keeping an eye on physical and moral safety (more on this shortly), *we are to turn our face toward everyone—not our back—and convey to them that God loves them.* We love them because, whatever else is going on in their lives, they were created in the image of the God we love.

… not willing for any to perish, but for all to come to repentance.
2 PETER 3:9

These people are held captive by God's enemy, carrying out his agenda—blinded, mis-informed, deceived—and therefore determined at some level to destroy, and devoted ultimately to destruction. This situation will continue unless each person perceives the love of the God they do not know, hears His invitation of relationship, and chooses to respond to His call—just as we have done.

Judgment is God's business. To extend His love to those outside His wall is our business … never knowing when even the one farthest down the road toward evil will turn to embrace God and accept His offer. *Should we not view these people as Jesus does?*

We may view those who engage in ungodly behaviors in many ways, and feel many things. Consider your personal experience. What is the difference between turning our back to someone and continuing to face them in these situations?

____

____

____

… to others show mercy mixed with fear—hating even the clothing stained by corrupted flesh.
Jude 1:23

Although they know God's righteous decree that those who do such things deserve death, they not only continue to do these very things but also approve of those who practice them.
Romans 1:32

The last scenario highlights the moral risk we face when we remain open to unbelievers. We must be careful to be guided by God's definition of love, *and not by Satan's re-definition of what it means to love.* In recent years, several of Satan's deceptions have melded together into a single concept: to love a person, as Christians intend to do, we must accept this person "*as they are.*" But this last phrase—"as they are"—has been redefined in a particular way.

That is, to *love*, we must necessarily accept, embrace, affirm, and celebrate all of a person's beliefs, choices, values, and appetites—for these are now viewed as *an integral part* and a valid expression of "who someone is as a person." According to this way of thinking, we do not truly accept a person unless we accept *everything about this person.* Thus, we cannot *truly love* someone if we refuse to "accept" any part of the entire package.

Can you spot several flaws in this line of thinking? Can we not truly love someone, yet deeply disagree with them on some point? Our society tells us that we cannot.

How can we truly love a person, yet disagree with their choices and lifestyle? *Our choices do not define who we are in the core of our being* (which is fortunate for Christians as well). The truth is, at some point all of us will vigorously disagree with anyone we truly love—whether this is a child, a friend, or a spouse. Does God truly love us? Does He disagree with anything about our lives? Instead of ignoring or embracing things that are wrong, the most loving thing we can do is to *speak the truth in love.*

Do you see the clever strategy in play here, when Satan tries to make unconditional love synonymous with "unconditional acceptance"? **First, Satan is trying to compromise believers.** How? By getting believers who truly care about someone to affirm and endorse ungodly behaviors *in the name of accepting/loving this person.* Some people intend to "win over" those who rebel against God by "loving" in this way. Instead, those who try this approach have already been "won over," for they now affirm/embrace/celebrate something that is morally wrong. People who do not love God are eager to influence those who do love Him, by persuading them to accept their beliefs (which, in reality, represent Satan's agenda).

There is grave danger in agreeing with the enemy's ideas. When we do so, we open the doorway to our inner being, and these ideas now become *our ideas.* These ideas influence our lives in many ways, in addition to compromising our relationship with the God we say that we serve … whom we now offend. If we say, "God's directives do not really matter," this is like saying that our two year old should play in the middle of a busy street, then joining them.

Second, Satan is trying to build a higher wall around those who might peer over his wall and see a real offer of a better life. Satan contends that, "God does not and cannot really love us, nor can those who embrace His beliefs." According to "the world," those who embrace God's truths, who condemn inherently destructive behaviors or simply refuse to affirm such things, stand in the way of everyone's freedom, which Satan assures us is the path to our best life. Satan, instead, affirms our ungodly desires and encourages us to violate God's prohibitions in any way we choose, as he did with Eve.

So, who really loves us, God or Satan? God offers us true life. The world insists that we—in the name of a distorted view of love—accept immoral and destructive behaviors. Some choices are not acceptable to God, nor should they be to us. At the same time, we are not to turn our backs on those who are struggling. We seek a balance: loving the sinner while hating the sin.

But the Pharisees and the teachers of the Law muttered,
"This man welcomes sinners and eats with them."
LUKE 15:2

Our model is Jesus. He viewed us as lost sheep—misguided, misdirected, dangerous to ourselves and others—yet still worthy of attention and effort because we were created in the image of God. Though people may continue to wander, **we remain devoted to their well-being—which in the end can only be found by hearing God's offer and embracing the Lordship of Christ.**

Christ-followers are to be fountains of living water, not walls of stone thrown up before those we deem to be unworthy.

Instead, speaking the truth in love, we will grow to become in every respect the mature body of Him who is the head, that is, Christ.
Ephesians 4:15

Our challenge is to maintain our integrity before the Lord as we extend His love to a lost and dying world—and to our brothers and sisters who stray from His ways. What are your thoughts on how we are to love others in these ways?

"OUR LIFE" WITHIN THE KINGDOM OF GOD

Frankly, most of us enter a relationship with God with this idea: "My life, made better." **We want God to fix our life.** Our world has trained us to pursue our beliefs, preferences, desires, and agenda as if our very life depends on having what we *think* we want and need ... **and we want to enlist God's help**. One of the greatest life lessons is realizing how little we understand about what we really need.

God, in contrast, knows exactly what we need. And He has in view the needs of everyone around us as well. There is no concept more powerful than realizing that my best life is not about my life, which in reality no longer exists. What if we began to view God's interests, desires, agenda, and plan in their proper light, versus our view from our limited vantage point?

We spoke earlier of the "Competing Kingdoms" model of marriage versus the Covenant model.

How does our full acceptance of the Lordship of Christ relate to our recognition that "my life"—my kingdom, over which I used to rule—no longer exists?

What if we grasped the reality of our connection with our brothers and sisters in Christ—and what this truly means? What happens to one of us happens to all of us. We are all part of a single body, and responsible for everyone's well-being. Does Scripture teach that this relationship exists? Did early Christians recognize this reality?

All the believers were together and held everything in common. They sold property and possessions to give to anyone who had need.
ACTS 2:44, 45

All the believers were one in heart and mind. No one claimed that any of their possessions were their own, but they shared everything they had ... And God's grace was so powerfully at work in them all that there were no needy persons among them.

ACTS 4:32-34

THE THINGS OF LIFE ARE FREELY SHARED, OR HELD IN COMMON

These verses clearly depict Covenant principles being lived out among early Christians. These principles obviously pertain to material goods. But "sharing in another's life" goes further. Scripture makes it clear that we are in a family relationship with God and with our (aptly termed) brothers and sisters in Christ. What does God expect of us in these relationships? See His "New Commandment" for details, and all the principles and practices of Covenant. **This is what God wants us to be toward each other.**

* * * * *

Rather than a list of questions at this point, please go back to the outline of our Covenant responsibilities (page 34-35) and the checklist of things that align with God's love (page 42-43). Consider current views and practices within the Christian community in light of God's intent for relationships within His Body. And consider your personal views and practices. No Christian individual or group has ever attained the fullness of God's intent on this earth, nor will they. God does not realistically expect perfection. What *does* He expect? He expects us to progressively shift our lives into alignment with His life and His directions.

As you consider God's intent, please consider how you can move toward His truth, His intent for His body of believers, and His plan for your life ... one step at a time. As you consider these things, what is your next step?

___

___

___

___

___

___

___

___

___

CHAPTER FOUR

THE NEW COVENANT: OUR UNSOLVABLE PROBLEMS AND JESUS' ANSWER

We have considered how God intends that we treat each other within a Covenant, and why we should do so. There are many other aspects, realities, and dimensions of this relationship that we must understand to truly live within this relationship as God desires. And, as we should desire, if we understood *why* God desires these things from us and for us. When we consider all that God asks us to be toward each other—in light of how we currently conduct our relationships—do we have more questions?

God asks for consistent love, unremitting faithfulness, and an unshakable commitment to honor others. So let us do a quick inventory of what is going on within us—in our minds and hearts—and what consistently comes out of us in our words and actions. How much of what goes on within us is about love, faithfulness, or honor? Then, we add words like consistently, unremitting, unshakable … Well, for at least some of us, our first question might be, "How do we get from here to there?

Through our *entry into Covenant,* God makes every change, lays every foundation, and provides every resource necessary for us to emulate His life in every detail that our finiteness allows. Every provision is already made for us to become loving and faithful, as God directs. It is now possible to worship Him with every fiber of our being. This potential is present. In any situation, the correct God-ordained, God-pleasing choice is possible for each of us. *A life that is radically transformed into the image of Christ is now possible for each of us.* This outcome is clearly God's desire for us. But we come back to the same question: How?

God paints a picture of extremes in Scripture: a kingdom of darkness versus a kingdom of light; the "old man/woman" versus "the new man/woman"; old life versus new life; the world versus the Kingdom of God; the flesh versus the Spirit; love versus not-love; obedience versus rebellion. All of these refer to the war in the heavens between God and His enemy, a war that has spilled over into our world and our lives.

God depicts our relationship with Him in terms of our life shifting from one extreme to the other. By entering Covenant with God, we proclaim our intention to divorce ourselves from God's enemy. By accepting Jesus as our Lord, we embrace our responsibility to walk away from the realm, behaviors, and leadership of this enemy. Instead, we commit ourselves to follow God's ways in His kingdom. **This is the radical life-change to which we have committed ourselves.**

Yet all of us seem to be caught in the middle—between the ways of God and the ways of the world, between obedience and something less, between faithfulness and unfaithfulness, between love and something else. *Some of our ways* are in line with the Kingdom of God, but other ways are still in line with the kingdom of darkness.

As you survey your life—your beliefs, values, priorities, desires, and actions—how many of the things within you, and how many of the things that come forth from inside of you, align with God's Word, will, and plan for your life?

____

____

____

How do you view this situation in light of God's intent that we love as He loves, become consistently faithful, and live out His plan for our lives in every detail?

____

____

____

Would you say that you are caught somewhere in the middle, between the life God holds out before us and our "old life"? If so, how would you explain this reality?

____

____

____

What we choose to do next, in light of this reality, has an inestimable impact on the rest of our earthly life and our eternity. How do we view this situation? What can we do about it? What should we do about it? What do we want to do about it? Most important: "What is God's plan, what does He want for us, and what has He made possible for us?" **These are the answers to the question: "How?"**

Much of the New Testament is directed toward people who have one foot firmly planted in the Kingdom of God, but the other foot … somewhere else (Ephesians 4:17–5:20). **Please note: God never says this situation is okay.** Why? Because He loves us and wants the best for us. Because He went to amazing lengths to provide for a new, different, and much better life for us—here and now as well as in eternity. Because He will call us to account one day for the new life He gave us and the opportunities He offered us—and whether we make something of these opportunities, or waste them.

Therefore, do not let sin reign in your mortal bodies so that you obey its evil desires. Do not offer any part of yourself to sin as an instrument of wickedness, but rather offer yourselves to God as those who have been brought from death to life; and offer every part of yourself to Him as an instrument of righteousness.
ROMANS 6:12, 13

Just as you received Christ Jesus as Lord, continue to live your lives in Him.
COLOSSIANS 2:6

OUR NEXT DECISION: WILL WE BE FAITHFUL TO OUR COVENANT?

Regarding Covenant, there are two fundamental decisions we must make. **First, do we choose to enter the New Covenant** when this offer is made clear to us? If so, all the changes we have described and the obligations we incur are fully in place. All the potential within this relationship is fully in place.

But there is a second decision as well. ***How do we respond to the commitments inherent in this relationship?*** Will we be faithful to our Covenant with God? And if we purpose to do so, will we faithfully live out this commitment in thought, word, and deed for the rest of our lives? **God intends that we both enter this relationship and remain faithful to our relationship and to Him.** In fact, it is embracing *our commitment to these commitments* that spurs us onward to life-change and maturity in Christ. Or we can remain indecisive, uncommitted, and confused about our responsibilities. In this case, will we remain stuck in the middle?

Who should we follow? To whom should we entrust our lives? How committed should we be? *Perhaps the best questions are: "How committed are we right now, and why?"*

In order to truly enter the New Covenant, we must engage in a life-for-life exchange with God. He gives us His life, and we give Him ours. Inherent in this is turning from our lordship over our life and the lordship of God's enemy to … what? *What commitment did we actually make* when we called Jesus our Lord?

Making a commitment and _keeping_ a commitment are different things. We may intend to keep our commitment, but many factors influence the extent to which we back our words with our actions. In fact, _our level of commitment to our commitments_ can vary widely. Some turn aside quickly; others will get the job done or die trying. What level of commitment does Covenant call for? The key questions are: _"What is our level of commitment to our commitment to make Jesus our Lord?"_ And, _"Why is this our answer?"_

Consider, for the rest of this volume, *who Jesus is, what He has done, why He has done these things, and what He has offered us.* Then look in the mirror. Consider who we now are within Covenant, what God asks of us, why He asks these things, and what we should offer back to God in return for all He has done for us.

God designed Covenant to solve a serious problem: the discrepancy between *what God requires versus what we are and the ways we choose to live.*

JESUS: SON OF GOD, SON OF MAN

Let's take another look at the exchange of life within Covenant. Jesus, as God, offers us the opportunity to share His life. As He often does, He leads the way by first sharing in our life. This is why we celebrate Christmas.

As we consider the extent to which the Living God shared in our frail and mortal lives, what does God want us to grasp? **He wants us to understand the extent to which He wants us to take on and live out His life, here and now.**

What do you believe it means to "take on and live out" the life of Christ?

WHY DID JESUS HAVE TO BECOME A HUMAN BEING?

Several ideas have been set forth as to why Jesus took on the fullness of our humanity. One is: "So He could communicate with us better." Or, so He could "understand us better." But the obvious reason is because of Covenant. **He came to earth to engage in an exchange of life with each of us.** And there was still another reason: He needed to die for our sins—which, if He was only God, would not be possible.

Consider the following:

- Jesus became fully human while remaining fully God.
- His earthly mother carried Him while under suspicion for immoral conduct.
- While we romanticize the place Jesus was born in Christmas celebrations, his first stop outside the womb was a cattle feed trough. Consider this option for your first child and why you might prefer almost any other option.
- He grew to physical maturity under the authority of human parents in a small, poor village of perhaps one hundred people. His life was unnoticed for almost thirty years.
- He needed to sleep and eat, and became tired, hungry, and thirsty like the rest of us.
- Though speaking the most pure truth ever heard by human ears, He was ignored, discounted, and maligned by those who claimed to be the most zealous worshippers of the God who now stood before them.
- He was subjected to disdain, malice, brutality, slander, and betrayal … by His chosen people, for whom He was willing to give His life.
- Then He was sentenced to torture and death by a reluctant Roman leader. The sentence was carried out by Roman soldiers who were, in contrast, enthusiastic torturers and executioners, who delighted in mocking the Creator of all things.
- Jesus was beaten so brutally that He was too weak to carry His cross to the site of His execution. A passerby was pressed into service to carry His cross for Him.
- He was stripped naked in a very public place, then subjected to perhaps the most bloody, slow, and excruciatingly painful form of execution ever devised.
- Beyond all of this, He underwent a pain beyond anything we could understand when His connection of "oneness" with His Father was ruptured. He underwent not just a physical death but also a spiritual separation from His Father as He "took upon Himself"—and paid for—the sins of those who would turn to Him.

Why did Jesus become all of this, and take on, all these things?

Then the Father raised Him from the dead. He became the "firstborn from the dead" (Colossians 1:18). Again, He led the way. In turn, we follow this same pattern of death and rebirth into a new, eternal, indestructible life (Romans 6:4, Hebrews 7:16).

Jesus replied, "Very truly I tell you, no one can see the Kingdom of God unless they are born again."
JOHN 3:3

We were therefore buried with Him through baptism into death in order that, as Christ was raised from the dead through the glory of the Father, we too may live a new life.
ROMANS 6:4

WHY DO WE HAVE TO DIE, THEN BE REBORN, TO ENTER THE NEW COVENANT?

This leads to a vital question. When we enter the New Covenant, we become an entirely *new creature* following a *new birth.* So what happened to the "old me"? When we come before God to accept His offer of relationship in the New Covenant, we offer Him our lives in return. What does He do next? He first puts our "old self" to death. Then we are raised to new life in a way analogous to Jesus' resurrection, with a completely new identity. But … why? *Why doesn't He just forgive us?*

If someone asked you why we need to die to enter the New Covenant, how would you answer—or, do you believe this language to be simply a metaphor?

____

____

____

WHAT IS OUR IDENTITY … THAT CHANGES AS WE ENTER COVENANT?

Before going further, we must consider another question: "What is our identity?" There are many parts of *us.* The best way to think of our identity is: all the fixed things about us that were created by God, that *we cannot change.* These include our spiritual gifts, our potential in various areas, and our wiring system. How much intellectual, artistic, or athletic potential do we have? We can choose to develop our potential, but we cannot create more potential than we were born with. Are we an extrovert or introvert, a visual learner or an auditory learner? **Our identity encompasses all the things about us that *simply are.*** Our identity, then, **can be contrasted with all the parts of ourselves that *we can change***—things like beliefs, preferences, feelings, desires, values, and character qualities.

How would you describe the difference between the various parts of your inner self? How would you contrast your identity with your emotions, beliefs, character, preferences, values, or self-image?

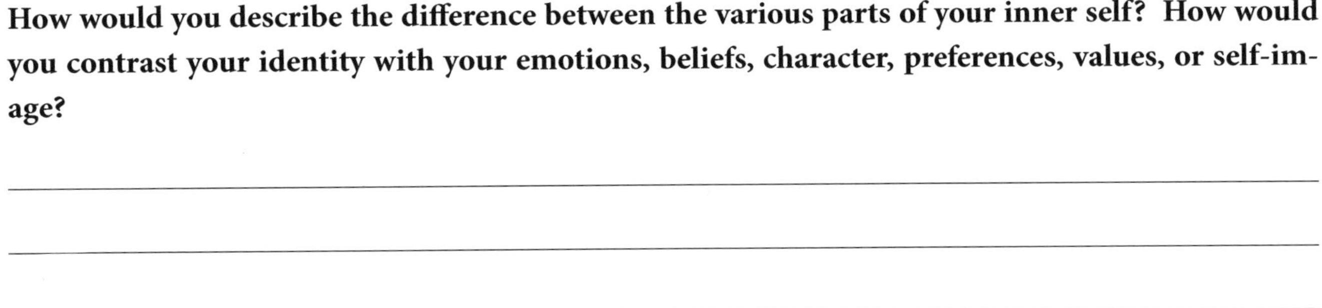

Those who live according to the sinful nature have their minds set on what that nature desires ... the mind of sinful man is death ... the sinful mind is hostile toward God. It does not submit to God's law, nor can it do so. Those controlled by the sinful nature cannot please God.
ROMANS 8:5-8

WHY DID OUR "OLD SELF" NEED TO DIE TO ENTER GOD'S KINGDOM?

From a Christian perspective, there is another way to think about our identity. Before entering the New Covenant, we had a "nature problem"—an element of us often termed a *sin nature.* This aspect of nature was passed down from Adam and Eve, who in turn acquired this aspect of nature from ... whom? We will discuss that question farther down. Simply note for now that this *nature problem* cannot be solved by any means *by us* (see the above passage). No decision or act of will on our part can overcome our rebellious nature toward God. Therefore, this element of self must be part of our identity—**the part of ourselves that we cannot change**. This is why we need a Savior, and why God needed to offer us more than forgiveness if we are to enter His Kingdom. We need an *entirely new identity/essence/nature* if we are to properly relate to God.

OUR MOST FUNDAMENTAL PROBLEM ...

The complete inability to obey and please God due to our "sin nature" is our most fundamental problem before we enter the New Covenant. Even if we do good things, our nature makes us incapable of wholehearted obedience to God. We may do *right things*, but for wrong reasons—just like the Pharisees.

It is helpful to consider what happened in the Garden of Eden, for these realities speak directly to our lives today. Adam and Eve were created "in the image of God." That is, both were created in a shared identity, or "oneness" (Covenant) relationship with God. Eve was also created in a "one-flesh" (Covenant) relationship with Adam.

If Adam and Eve could not change their nature, what could change it—and at the same time rupture their oneness with God? They could commit "spiritual adultery" against God—by believing, believing in, and entrusting their future to God's enemy. They attested to this shift of *lordship* by turning from

God to embrace, then act out the agenda of God's enemy. They broke their Covenant with God—and at the same time entered a covenant with His enemy. How can we know that this occurred?

This scenario parallels marital adultery. If a person engages in sexual intercourse outside of his or her marriage, a new covenant is forged as the former Marriage Covenant is broken. God allows divorce when adultery occurs because the original one-flesh state has been replaced with another one-flesh relationship. **In truth, a new covenant is already in force.**

Consider the vast shift in our society's view of sexual activity. Over the last seventy years we have attempted to separate this activity from the commitments of Marriage. How does our society's view today differ from God's view?

____

____

____

Do you note any parallel between the widespread lack of faithfulness to the commitments inherent in Marriage Covenants that are being created by sexual activity in our society and a widespread lack of faithfulness to the commitments inherent in the New Covenant in our current Christian culture? In what ways does a lack of understanding of Covenant impact lives?

____

____

____

When Adam and Eve's *oneness with God* disappeared, **so did their citizenship in His paradise.** They were ejected from Eden. The unending life they were created to enjoy **was replaced with a slow march toward physical death**. They were now *one* with their new lord—sharing his "sin nature" within his "kingdom of darkness" (Colossians 1:13).

This has been the starting point of every human life ever since. **Embedded within our identity is a nature that innately rebels against our Creator.** Thus, we all await the decreed sentence of death as payment for our sins (Genesis 2:17; Romans 3:23, 6:23).

In part, this sentence has already been carried out. The term *death* in the original Hebrew simply means "separation." **Here this term has a twofold meaning: first, physical death**—the separation of our soul from our body; **second, our separation from God.** We all begin life separated from our Creator. But there is more to come. **The ultimate death is eternal separation from God** (I Thessalonians 1:9)—in a place of unending torment, and in the company of the master we continue to prefer above God (Satan and his followers)—if we refuse God's offer to enter the New Covenant.

You were dead because of your sins and because your sinful nature was not yet cut away. Then, God made you alive with Christ, for He forgave all your sins.
COLOSSIANS 2:13

Your whole self ruled by the flesh was put off when you were circumcised by Christ.
COLOSSIANS 2:11

Our most fundamental problem, then, is twofold: first, a nature that drives us to sin; second, rebellious acts against God in accordance with our nature. No choice or act of our will on our part can overcome this problem. Only God can save us. Fortunately, He offers to do so. How does God's Covenant plan address these two issues? We shall see.

CHAPTER FIVE

THE NEW COVENANT: GOD'S PLAN TO RESCUE AND RESTORE US

To reverse the changes that occurred in the Garden, we simply reverse the process followed by Adam and Eve. Adam and Eve heard a false sales pitch for a better life—"you will become 'like God"—which certainly sounded like a life-upgrade (Genesis 3:5). They could enjoy this wonderful future … but only if they would rebel against their Creator.

Adam and Eve were faced with a credibility question. Who should they believe: God or Satan? They chose to believe Satan—and agree with him that God's command and promised consequence were lies. They chose to believe that Satan's offer was genuine. They affixed *their hope for their best life* to Satan's false promise. That is, they chose to *believe in Satan*—and place their lives and their future in his hands.

We are now presented with a similar, though true, offer of a new and better life (John 17:20). We must hear God's offer, believe His offer to be true (John 5:24), then believe in Him (John 3:36). That is, we must *recognize who He is—His power, His love, and His faithfulness to do as He has promised.* Then we must receive Him as our Lord and Savior (Romans 10:9-13), accepting His offer of relationship and all that this involves (John 1:12). *We commit our lives to Him, and offer our lives to Him.*

But the same credibility question still lingers. For Satan's most fundamental lie—first conveyed to humanity in the Garden—still impacts all of our lives. What is this lie? He tells us that **a life spent following his leadership is better—more exciting, fulfilling, gratifying—than a life "constrained" by God's rules.** Satan comes—so he claims—to "set us free."

And he does, in fact, "set us free" … from a proper relationship with God and the blessings of God. He offers "a better life." Instead, his path leads only to damage, destruction, and death. **Despite this, his sales pitch remains oddly compelling.** It is crucial to examine Satan's sales campaign: his character and the agenda behind this campaign. If we don't, **we will be drawn to this same promise of "a better life" ... if only we will turn from God's path.**

How do you feel about being *too committed* to God, *too different* from our culture, and too quick to turn from the "delights" of our current world?

____

____

____

If we are reluctant to *totally turn away* from the things of this world, why is this?

____

____

____

To enter Covenant with God we must turn to God and divorce ourselves from the lord of this world and the ways of his world. **Are we truly convinced that this was/is our best move?** If we are not, and continue to find the words of the "father of lies" credible, we will remain stuck in the middle, trying to walk down two paths that lead in opposite directions. **Or, we could take the time to figure out who loves us and always tells the truth, and who lies incessantly and is devoted to our destruction.**

"Bring forth fruit in keeping with repentance." —John the Baptist
LUKE 3:8

WHAT DOES IT MEAN TO REPENT?

In Scripture, turning from Satan/the world to God is termed *repentance* (Acts 2:38, 3:19). The Greek word so translated simply means to turn 180 degrees and walk in the opposite direction. Our walk *with* God means we walk *directly toward Him*, and *directly away from* the world and its ways. **Repentance means we are to stop living as we did previously and start living in ways that reflect God's life and Kingdom.**

To produce what He intends through the New Covenant, **God's Covenant Plan relies on our faithfulness.** Let us briefly review what it means to be in Covenant with God.

- Through "receiving" the blood/life of Christ we receive a new identity, an eternal life that is re-made in God's image (Ephesians 4:24).

- Through the life-exchange of Covenant, *Christ makes Himself liable for our debts.* Christ's death can now serve as payment for our sin-debt to God. The death of our "old self" mirrors Christ's death, and our "new birth" mirrors His resurrection. Notice, too, that these exchanges are not the end point of Covenant. These exchanges are merely the first of many that God intends.

- Through the exchange of natures between God (the Holy Spirit, now within us) and our new nature, which now resides within Christ, we return to a relationship of "oneness" with God. Thus, we became an *extension of each other's life.*

- Thus, we are transferred out of the kingdom of darkness that is ruled by the prince of this world, and into God's Kingdom to live eternally (John 17:14). We are no longer under any compulsion to obey Satan (Romans 6:6). We vowed instead to install God in this command/control role in our lives.

IS WHOLEHEARTED FAITHFULNESS TO GOD EVEN POSSIBLE?

One more consequence of entry into the New Covenant needs to be discussed in some detail, for there is much confusion about this vital point. **In order to be faithful in the ways God intends, we must realize that such faithfulness is actually possible.** In contrast, most current teaching implies that such faithfulness *is not* possible.

A KEY QUESTION: DO CHRISTIANS STILL HAVE A "SIN NATURE"?

There are two opinions about this among Christian teachers and theologians. The majority opinion seems to be: "Yes, we do." But neither God nor reality are swayed by our opinions. I believe both Scripture and the nature of Covenant say: "No, we do not."

Consider why the answer is important from a personal perspective. People will simply not expend vast amounts of effort trying to do something they know is impossible. Why bring up this obvious point? Because **we can all agree that we remain imperfect as Christians.** On occasion, we do things we know violate God's instructions. Or we may not know what God desires. In either case, by *sinning* we depart from the wisest possible instructions to build our best possible life. So one must ask: ***"Why do we not follow God perfectly once we are a Christian?"***

Here, the "sin nature" question become important. ***How we understand the source of our imperfections once we are a Christian will determine <u>what we do about</u> those imperfections—or what we <u>refrain from doing</u>.***

That is, our faithfulness—*our degree of commitment* to our commitment to God—will be determined by *<u>what we believe</u>*. If we have a clear understanding of who we now are, and the plan and resources God has provided for us within Covenant, we will find that we are well equipped to do as God requires. But what if we believe that wholehearted obedience to God is not a choice we can possibly make … because our "nature" still does not allow us to do so?

WHICH "SIN NATURE" ANSWER ALIGNS WITH SCRIPTURE AND COVENANT?

Let us consider both answers to the "sin nature" question in light of what we already know about *our nature* and Covenant. Then we will examine what Scripture teaches.

ANSWER #1: WE STILL HAVE A SIN NATURE.

- If so, **we cannot overcome this force within us by any choice or act of will.** It is therefore impossible for us to consistently obey God, or please Him—or love Him. We may make superficial changes, but the quest to fully obey God, or to love as He loves, or live as He lives is absolutely beyond our reach. So why even try to do so? Perhaps this is why so many Christian lives bear so much resemblance to their old life, and to the lives of the non-Christians around us.

- How does one who believes Answer #1 deal with God's call to live a new and different life? How does one handle the discrepancy between what God says to do, and how we live? **The real answer to this discrepancy—in this way of thinking—is not comprehensive life-change (which is imagined to be impossible)**. Instead, the real answer is "God's grace, mercy, and forgiveness." It is implied that God doesn't really expect us to obey His directions, nor should we expect this of (or for) ourselves. We are simply to be content that we are saved! For extra credit, we can acknowledge how much of a sinner we really are. Who, then, is going to fix our messed-up lives?

- In this way of thinking, God is responsible for any change in in our inner being, or in the way we live. Life-change becomes a "God thing," not an "us thing." Or, conversely, **He is accountable for any lack of change in us**. Which relieves us of accountability as we continue to be (what we think of as) "ourselves," and continue to behave in ways that violate God's directions.

If Answer #1 is true, *my way of life is not really my choice*. Instead, it is an "authentic expression of who I am/who God made me to be" plus "my sin nature." **If God wants me to be different, He must change me. Until then …**

Please note: People who believe in this way never hold out as a realistic expectation the radical life-change described in Scripture.

ANSWER #2: WE NO LONGER HAVE A SIN NATURE.

- If so, **obedience at any point is now an option we can choose**. These are the choices God instructs us to make, then expects us to make.

- If this is the case, **we still must understand why we depart from God's path with some regularity**. But now we have a workable plan to deal with the discrepancy between the ways God says to live and the ways we choose to live. This problem now rests squarely on our shoulders. We can make the choice to change our lives.

- If this is the case, **the life God holds out before us in Scripture and urges us to live now becomes an attainable objective in every detail.** The path to this life is obviously a process that involves growth toward maturity in Christ.

- Some kind of inner transformation is still required, in addition to the one God accomplished as we entered Covenant. What must change, and how does this occur?

We must first identify the source of our inner resistance to God and His plan—which Scripture terms *evil desires* (I Peter 1:14; II Peter 1:4; James 1:14; I Corinthians 10:6; Galatians 5:17). These evil desires are obviously present within Christians. But from where do these arise? There are two key insights: first, these desires *can change*. Therefore, these cannot arise from our identity, or nature, but must arise from another part of us. Second, an evil desire is *a desire in harmony with the source of all evil*—Satan. We *chose to want* what *Satan tells us to want,* versus what God tells us to want.

Why do we desire something? Because we believe it will enhance our lives. Desires occur first in our mind as we buy into the idea that something is beneficial. But we can rescind and re-make this decision. We will talk much more about this process, for it is vital to understand. **In brief, God's plan for this "second transformation" within Covenant deals with *the parts of our inner self that we can change.*** This process requires our active and devoted involvement.

...be transformed by the renewing of your minds...
Romans 12:2

If Answer #2 is correct, the real questions are: **1) what about us did change when we entered Covenant?; 2) what about us did not change at that time?; 3) what about us still needs to change to come into alignment with the life of God?; and 4) how do these still-needed changes occur?**

THE "SIN NATURE" QUESTION IN LIGHT OF COVENANT REALITIES

If we are seeking truth, only the answers within Scripture matter. Still, the realities of Covenant, then simple logic and common sense, are worth noting.

- In the Garden our connection with God was ruptured. His presence within Adam and Eve departed, for He must *re-enter us* in the New Covenant. In a way analogous to the Covenant of Marriage, **we can only be "one" with one God (or god) at a time.**

- "Satan in, God out" was the reality in Eden; and now **"God in, Satan out" is our reality as a consequence of entering the New Covenant.**

- We are now the "temple of the Holy Spirit" (I Corinthians 6:19). **Is God going to "share a room" with His enemy?**

- We are now within the Kingdom of God (Colossians 1:13). **Is God going to invite the spirit of His enemy to reside within His Kingdom?**

- When we enter the New Covenant, our death is required, not just forgiveness. Colossians 2:13 (cited earlier) notes that we were dead because of our sins, and because our sinful nature was not yet cut away. Here, both of our "insolvable problems" are cited—our nature and our resulting actions. Two verses earlier in Colossians (2:11 noted above), it notes that *this nature part was "circumcised away"* by Christ. **This verse makes two things synonymous: our death (or separation from God) and the presence of a sin nature.**

- Thus, if we are to have a new life—one no longer separated from God—**this appears to require the absence of Satan's rebellious nature.**

- The definition of being *one* with another, of being in Covenant with another, *is the mutual sharing of natures.* If we continue to have Satan's nature within us as a Christian, **this means that we must now be "one" with both God and Satan. Further, if Satan is still within us, and we are within Christ, what does this mean? While Satan welcomes confusion at this point, God clearly does not.**

THE "SIN NATURE" QUESTION ANSWERED IN GOD'S WORD

Now let us turn to the Scriptures. What change occurred as we entered Covenant?

> *For we know that our old self was crucified with Him so that the body ruled by sin might be done away with, that we should no longer be slaves to sin.*
>
> ROMANS 6:6

In Him you were also circumcised with a circumcision not performed by human hands. Your whole self ruled by the flesh was put off when you were circumcised by Christ.
COLOSSIANS 2:11

As a urologist, I have performed many circumcisions. **What is circumcised no longer remains a part of the person**. No one has ever left my office with this body-part still in their possession. When someone is crucified, they die—or are "done away with," as stated in Romans 6:6. ***What goes away, according to Scripture, when we enter the New Covenant?*** The "old self," the "body ruled by sin," the "whole self ruled by the flesh," and, stated most precisely, "our sinful nature" (Colossians 2:13).

In doing this, God completes the sentence imposed in Genesis 2:17. Our old "original self"—polluted by the nature of God's enemy, rebellious by nature, unable to be brought into alignment with Him—***is removed and obliterated.*** This identity/nature/life is replaced by an entirely new life which arises from a new birth that parallels Jesus' resurrection.

We have probably all been taught at some point that we continue to have a "sin nature" as a Christian. In light of the above, do you believe this?

____

____

____

Why does your answer matter?

____

____

____

THE PRACTICAL CONSEQUENCES OF THE "SIN NATURE" QUESTION

We pose the question about a sin nature for one vastly important reason. Either God has changed us by entry into Covenant so that we are capable of choosing to obey Him at any point—and love like He loves; or, once we are a Christian, the changes God worked within us are *still insufficient* to enable us to choose to obey Him at every point.

The truth of this matter is vital for day-to-day life. If obedience and faithfulness are now solely our responsibility, and a responsibility we can fulfill by choice and effort with God's help, **we can approach the discrepancy between our life and the life God says to live anticipating success—and achieving it by following God's plan.**

If, instead, we deem the necessary choices and life-transformation **not to be** our responsibility, **and deem any effort in that direction on our part to be futile, what effort will we make?** I have spoken with far too many people who believe this to be the case, and their lives have suffered as a result.

How do you view the discrepancy between the life God calls us to live and our current life? Why are we not fully obedient to God?

____

____

____

Who is responsible for adjusting our life and bringing it into alignment with God's life and will?

____

____

____

What choices must we make if this is to occur? That is: What is God's plan within Covenant so that we can do and be and become what God desires?

____

____

____

The actual answer to the last question may come as a surprise, for it involves far more than applying our willpower to "say no to sin," or to "make better decisions."

DOES GOD "DO IT ALL" … EVER?

An unfortunate byproduct of the "life change is a God thing/I can't change who I am" mindset **is a sweeping misconception of our role in our relationship with God.** In this way of thinking God plays every active role. We humans are merely passive, though grateful recipients of all that He does. There is a grain of truth in this, for God is many things we are not, and He does many things we cannot do. He calls the shots and determines the outcomes. He has the plan. We could not save ourselves, and we cannot properly lead or conduct our lives apart from His truth and His active input. All of this is true, and more.

However, none of this means that we *do nothing* … ever. The idea that our proper role is to be merely a passive recipient is perhaps the most dangerous misconception spread within the body of Christ. Why? Because this belief *ensures our lack of faithfulness based on the lack of a commitment we never realized we needed to make.*

Consider this concept within another Covenant: marriage. For a few months try taking no initiative whatsoever in your marriage. Simply be a grateful recipient of all that your spouse does. How's that working out for you? Not well, if this is what you actually do. Instead, Covenant is an "all in," reciprocal, *"takes everything we have, and we keep having to learn how to do it better"* kind of thing—if we are to build our relationship and ourselves to their potential.

Regarding the role we play to enter the New Covenant, the soundbite often used is: "Before God saved us we were dead, and dead people cannot do anything." We were dead—in the sense of being separated from God—but we were not inactive as if we were simply laying in a coffin. We were very active—apart from God, and in opposition to Him. **This was the problem. This life is why we need to repent, and why Jesus needed to die on a Roman cross.**

Even when it comes to entering the New Covenant, we do not "do nothing." If this is the case in our mind, we may not have actually entered this relationship with God. Covenant is a voluntary life-for-life exchange. **To enter Covenant, we must offer our life to the other and receive their life in return. We engage in a transaction that involves our mind, heart, and will.**

To enter the New Covenant, we make choices. Then **we commit ourselves to faithfully back up these choices** with myriad other choices for the rest of our time on earth. We also do not "give nothing" to enter the New Covenant. It is true that we do not earn or purchase this opportunity. God alone engineers this opportunity and offers it to us. On the other hand, **we must give God two things: 1) our agreement to receive His life on His terms; 2) in return, we agree to give our life to Him, to do with as He pleases.**

Recall the point in time when you accepted Christ's offer of the New Covenant. Did you adopt some new idea as your own, make a choice, and make a commitment? Do you now better understand God's terms to enter this relationship? Would you like to take a moment before the Lord to reaffirm your commitment, or to modify the commitment you made to Him, and bring it into alignment with His actual offer? Then, to take some time to worship our inconceivably wonderful and loving Heavenly Father? Record any thoughts here.

From that time on Jesus began to preach and say, "Repent [change your inner self—your old way of thinking, regret past sins, live your life in a way that proves repentance, seek God's purpose for your life], for the Kingdom of Heaven is at hand."
MATTHEW 4:17 (AMPLIFIED BIBLE)

THE SUCCESS OF GOD'S COVENANT PLAN DEPENDS ON OUR CHOICES

If we made these commitments, employing our mind, heart, and will at the entry point to this relationship, **our life will begin to turn 180 degrees and move in the opposite direction—toward God**. If we did not make these (necessary) commitments to God, where are our lives (still) headed?

If we never committed to change the direction of our life, and we remain confused about whom we want to follow … and our lives remain a confused mess … and we expect God to fix our life while we continue doing nothing … well, good luck with that. God offers a relationship with Himself on His terms … not ours.

Within a marriage, imagine if we remained confused about whom we married, and where we actually live—and act accordingly. What is needed here? Do we need to clarify the requirements of marriage, then make our own commitment in keeping with these requirements, then back up this commitment with our life? Perhaps we need to do the same in our relationship with God. Nothing less will do.

No temptation has seized you except what is common to humanity. And God is faithful; He will not let you be tempted beyond what you can bear. But when you are tempted, He will also provide an escape, so that you can stand up under it.
I CORINTHIANS 10:13 (BSB)

DO WE EVER HAVE "NO CHOICE"?

Consider the above verse. "Temptation" means that we are presented with the opportunity to engage in ungodly behavior, along with a seemingly plausible reason to do so, in conjunction with whatever desires may be kindled within us.

We must now make a choice. Do we choose to act in accord with the kingdom of darkness from which we came, or do we display our new citizenship in the Kingdom of God through our actions? **Or, in our minds, do we "have no choice but to … "**

Frankly, at times it feels like we have "no choice"—due to a strong inner inclination, a seemingly irresistible desire, or overwhelming external pressure. **God makes a remarkably important statement in the above verse.** In any situation, regardless of how we feel or what we think, if our most important priority is our relationship with God, we will always be able to resist any internal urge to depart from His path—through our firm decision to do so, plus all the willpower we can muster, perhaps aided in the moment by power from God Himself. **God's Word tells us that we can stand up against any internal or external pressure to sin, if we choose to do so.**

Equally important, we have God's assurance that **He will always provide an option in any scenario that aligns with His will**. So, no external circumstance can force us to sin. We literally never have "no choice." We do always have a choice. One option will always be to follow God. This is always our best option in the long run. We do get to choose. Do we bow to internal or external pressure, or do we bow our knee to God?

Everyone who turns from God's leadership will always have "their reasons." Consider your own history. What was going on in your mind and heart in these situations. What "reasons" do we base unfortunate decisions upon?

____

____

____

What good does it do, my brothers, if someone claims to have faith but does not prove it with his actions?
James 2:14 (Intl. Standard Version)

Therefore, I urge you, brothers and sisters, in view of God's mercy, to offer your bodies as a living sacrifice, holy and pleasing to God—this is your true and proper worship. Do not conform to the pattern of this world, but be transformed by the renewing of your mind. Then you will be able to test and approve what God's will is—His good, pleasing, and perfect will.
Romans 12:1, 2

WHY DO WE STILL STRAY FROM GOD AS A CHRISTIAN?

First, we remain confused about whom we want to follow. Whose leadership is truly best for us: God's or Satan's? We may be confused about the nature of the relationship we entered with God and the changes that have occurred within us.

But there is another reason that Scripture highlights at several points: our flesh. This aspect of our inner self is described as the source of our internal resistance to God's will, Word, and plan (Galatians 5:17). We will have much to say in coming chapters and future volumes about this source of resistance: what "the flesh" consists of, and how to successfully deal with its urge toward disobedience.

WHY DOES CONFUSION EXIST ABOUT THE PRESENCE OF A "SIN NATURE"?

In defense of those who believe Christians still possess a "sin nature," **confusion arises from the ways the term "the flesh" is used in the New Testament.** At times,"the flesh" is used to describe the totality of our mortal being: mind, heart, will, and body. Or, this term may specifically refer to our sin nature (e.g. Colossians 2:11). In other places it describes the source of our "sinful desires" after we become a Christian (Galatians 5:17). Or, the term "the flesh" may simply refer to our physical body.

If we view the flesh as a single, seamless entity that is the source of ungodliness within us (before and after we become a Christian), one could reasonably conclude that "the flesh" is synonymous with a "sin nature." If one starts with this assumption, one simply glosses over verses describing the removal of that nature, and Jesus' insistence that His followers be taught to obey *everything He commanded* (Matthew 28:20).

John Calvin, with little of the understanding of Covenant detailed in this volume, saw "the flesh" as a seamless whole, as the entirety of "us." Since a source of rebellion remains within us, Calvin concluded that this "entirety" must still be utterly, thoroughly corrupted by sin, even as a Christian. From these assumptions arose his "doctrine of total depravity." Much teaching today aligns with Calvin's thoughts on this point.

But there is another way to sort out this language that harmonizes better with both the rest of Scripture, and the realities of Covenant. The term "the flesh" certainly may refer to the totality of our living being, **but this term can also refer to *various parts* of our being**. Our inner being is comprised of parts **that came to be in different ways.** God's Covenant plan provides ***completely different solutions*** for problems that arise from these different parts.

For the "sin nature" problem within our old identity, God offers us a new life. This is 100 percent a work of God. But once this "nature problem" is solved via entry into Covenant, so we are no longer slaves to sin (Romans 6:6, 7), we are now free to choose to follow God. **Or, we remain free to choose not follow Him.** Now the issue becomes our faithfulness.

CHOOSING TO CHANGE OUR LIFE—HAND IN HAND WITH GOD

Our true self/identity may point our lives in one direction, **but other influences within us may point in other directions**. Our lives are directed by a collection of often-conflicting voices. As a Christian, our voice belongs to God's Spirit. He, along with the example of Jesus and the requirements of Covenant, speak with a single voice in harmony with God's Word. We may choose to follow this voice. Or we may choose instead to follow another internal voice. Scripture terms this *opposing voice "the flesh," which instead gives voice to evil desires.* From what part of us does this voice arise?

These desires do arise from the fabric of our being. But God calls us to effectively overcome this source of resistance in the interest of faithfulness. We are ultimately called to engage in a process of inner transformation—that progressively removes this influence, and replaces evil desires with a growing desire for God and the things of God (Romans 12:1, 2; Ephesians 4:22-24). None of this would be true if we were still faced with a "nature problem." ***If this inner voice does not arise from our new nature, where does it arise from?*** We will return to this question in a later chapter.

The topic of this workbook is God's love. We set forth a definition of "God's love." Then, we spent considerable time talking about faithfulness and obedience. The point was made earlier that, "We cannot have love without faithfulness and obedience." What are your thoughts on this statement?

____

____

____

Suppose you are struggling with a pattern of behavior that is out-of-sync with God's will. Perhaps this has to do with a character attribute, or a strong desire, or simply a habit that is hard to break. What have you been taught during your Christian life about the proper way to approach such problems?

____

____

____

How successful have you been thus far in putting away things that should not be in your life according to Scripture, or adding things that Scripture says should be a part of your life?

____

____

____

What has your experience been thus far with spiritual growth and life-change? Are you growing in Christ in the ways you believe you should be, or are you encountering roadblocks you have yet to overcome? What has produced the most growth in your life thus far, or what approaches have you tried that have yet to succeed as you grapple with life issues?

____

____

____

True or False: Any ongoing, serious struggle we experience while attempting to obey God is the result of the ongoing presence of a "sin nature." T____. F____.

CHAPTER SIX

THE GIFTS OF GOD: NEW LIFE ... AND HIS LIFE

...put on the new self, created to be like God in true righteousness and holiness.
EPHESIANS 4:22-24

HOW CAN WE CHARACTERIZE OUR NEW LIFE/IDENTITY?

Let us consider this **gift of life** we have received. **What is this life?** Our new life/identity/essence/nature mirrors the life of God—His righteousness and holiness. Our true self is made in His image, no longer tainted by the nature of His enemy.

His divine power has given us everything we need for a godly life through our knowledge of Him who called us by His own glory and goodness.
2 PETER 1:3

Our deepest *true self* is now in harmony with God's life. If we want to live an *authentic life*, how would we describe this life? We now have access to everything we need to live our best life before God. Our life now has vast new potential. This potential is just waiting to be developed. And all of this occurs through the "knowledge" of God.

WE KNOW GOD

The word *knowledge* means that we know things about Jesus, but this is also a Covenant term, as in "Adam knew his wife, and she conceived ... " (Genesis 4:1). We have what we need because we have entered *the most intimate possible relationship with God,* and we share in His life.

FREE FROM THE GRIP OF SATAN'S NATURE, WE CAN CHOOSE TO OBEY

We are no longer *slaves to sin* (Romans 6:6), compelled to do destructive things by our nature (Romans 7:14-20). Our inner being is washed clean and made altogether new. We can freely choose to follow God at any and every point (Matthew 28:20). We can now freely choose to love Him and serve Him (Hebrews 9:14).

WE ARE LED TO DO WHAT IS MOST BENEFICIAL FOR OURSELVES AND OTHERS

Christ instructs us to do what is most beneficial for ourselves and other people (Matthew 22:40), as did God's Law in the Old Testament (Matthew 7:12). We are to play the most constructive role in other people's lives and enjoy the blessings of doing so.

As we wake each morning and go about our day, are we keenly aware that God's will is the most beneficial guidance we could possibly have?

____

____

____

If we keep this reality in mind, what difference will it make?

____

____

____

OUR INNER AND OUTER LIFE: TRANSFORMING INTO THE IMAGE OF CHRIST

The shift from old life to new life is a lifelong, continuous process (Colossians 3:1-16). In the ways we have become "like Christ," we will build good things in life and accrue blessings. To the extent that we are "not there yet," we will continue to create problems for ourselves and others. God does not realistically expect perfection from us any more than I can expect my five-year-old to take out a diseased kidney. God does expect us to be attentive, devoted, and responsive. He expects us to be on the path toward Him.

"A disciple is not above his teacher, but everyone who is fully trained will be like his teacher."
LUKE 6:40

GROWING OUR NEW LIFE TO MATURITY: AN EXERCISE IN FAITHFULNESS

God describes the growth of our new life in terms of our initial journey to adulthood—infancy, childhood, growth, then maturity in Christ. I might expect my five-year-old to draw a picture of a kidney. After receiving the proper training—years later—I am very capable of removing one if the need arises.

God expects us to view every aspect of life as a part of our training process. We are to learn to follow Him and emulate His life in each detail. He expects us to develop the potential He placed within us—with the same wonder and enthusiasm we displayed as we learned to walk, ride a bike, read, drive a car—or take out a kidney.

No discipline seems pleasant at the time, but painful. Later on, however, it produces a harvest of righteousness and peace for those who have been trained by it.
HEBREWS 12:11

Do we view our life as *our circumstances*, or as *our training process*? Why would our viewpoint matter?

____

____

____

God places spiritual gifts within our new self. These are special abilities that allow us to perform various ministry functions within His Body. He intends that we take special care to develop and use these capabilities.

Have you identified your spiritual gifts? If so, what have you done to develop and use your gifts?

____

____

____

LIFE CHANGE RESULTS FROM BEING TRAINED, OR CORRECTLY TAUGHT

Notice the pattern: in His Great Commission, Jesus instructs His followers to teach the next and subsequent generations to *obey everything* He commanded. In Ephesians 4:22 (atop this chapter) we are taught to put off the old self and put on the new self. In the verse just above Jesus describes the path to becoming *like Him*: we must be *fully trained*. Then, in Hebrews 12:11 God notes that such training is not always pleasant.

Learning how to live well before the Lord, or to build a great marriage—these are among the most challenging tasks we will ever undertake. And the most rewarding—if we build as God instructs. The operative words are *decision, commitment,* and *effort.*

Consider this: "typical" church life in our culture involves, at most, a few hours per week. We attend meetings. We may spend time and energy in church programs or projects. But of our available 168 hours per week, what amount of time and energy do we devote to things that build our relationship with God? Has it occurred to us that everything we do and every ounce of energy we expend is to be devoted to God? Are we aware that God intends that we devote vast energy and time to building this relationship, and building ourselves into His image? What else might we do—in addition to church meetings and programs—to move toward these goals?

____

____

____

____

____

____

WHY CAN'T WE JUST SHOW UP AND DO WHAT WE FEEL LIKE DOING?

In Scripture, we do see the picture of just showing up with our new self, then doing whatever we feel like doing. **Note that "what we feel like doing" are the things we have always done.** These are our familiar, comfortable, predictable behaviors. We chose to do these things in the first place, and we have done them ever since. In other words, this is our "old life." God intends, instead, to pull us out of these comfortable, familiar, often counter-productive places and patterns. Are we willing to follow Him?

In our culture, maturity is not highly valued. "Adulting" is not desired by young minds. Why is this? Because becoming mature involves work, along with assuming and fulfilling responsibilities. Maturity means that we meet other's needs instead of just our own. What is behind the drive toward immaturity in our culture? Is immaturity truly the life we want? What are your thoughts?

____

____

____

AN EXCHANGE OF LIFE WITH GOD

But God has even more for us. Covenant is a life-for-life exchange. If we know God, beyond just enjoying our new life, **we have the opportunity to share in His life.** What does such sharing look like?

Within Covenant we may freely draw from His life: His peace, joy, and strength. Within Covenant we have access to *everything within His character and ability.* This may include doing miracles through His people, or for His people.

What of God's life would be of benefit in your life?

____

____

____

Through these He has given us His very great and precious promises,
so that through them you may participate in the divine nature …
having escaped the corruption in the world caused by evil desires.
2 Peter 1:4

My dear children, for whom I am again in the pains of childbirth until Christ is formed in you, how I wish I could be with you now and change my tone, because I am perplexed about you!
Galatians 5:19, 20

THE LIFE OF GOD WITHIN US

While our new life is a wonderful experience, at the same time we live in a world that continues to stretch us to the breaking point. We may face overwhelming circumstances. We may need resources beyond our own. We are joined to a Creator who has committed *His help* and *His life* to us. What can we expect from Him?

In Scripture God makes specific promises to us in this regard, but often with conditions. As we see above, the life God offers to us may not become evident in our lives. God's love is unconditional. But His blessings, access to the benefits and beauties of His life, and His treasures—these are contingent on our faithfulness. Two Covenant principles are in play here: first, the mutual nature of Covenant; second, the exchange of life within Covenant. **God continues to remind us that we must be faithful if we want to be blessed.** Covenant is an "all in" thing on both sides! God wants us to experience His life—but only if we meet certain conditions.

Be anxious for nothing, but in everything by prayer and supplication with thanksgiving make your request known to God, and the peace of God that surpasses all comprehension will guard your hearts and your minds in Christ Jesus.
PHILIPPIANS 4:6, 7

THE PROMISES OF GOD: "IF YOU DO THIS, I WILL DO THAT"

I became a Christian during my first year of medical school. The Holy Spirit was within me, but I was also filled with anxiety. Medical students are under unremitting pressure, having literally more material to cover than is humanly possible before each week's tests in every subject. My anxiety made it difficult for me to focus and assimilate what I was studying. I shared my struggle with a Christian friend. He pointed me to Philippians 4:6-7, then he said, "Do what God says in this verse, and watch what He does in response."

This was my introduction to God's many specific promises. *These are always phrased in the same way: "If you do this, I will do that."* God requires a display of obedience and faithfulness on our part, then offers a blessing in response.

The next time I began to feel overwhelmed by a pile of study materials, and a clock showing less time than needed to cover all of it, I put my studies aside and picked up my Bible. I read this passage and followed what God said to do, step by step.

God says several key things in this passage. First, how does He reference anxiety? With *a command not to be anxious for anything.* So, my first move is an *apology for disobeying His command* by being anxious. Second, I should pray about the topic of concern and request the desired outcome. Third, and perhaps most important, this request must be accompanied by giving thanks. **The first two items were easy, but the third one brought me to a stop.** All that came to mind were the reasons I was displeased and distressed. Nowhere in my mind was there any reason for thanksgiving.

As I struggled to find a reason to "give thanks," it was as if a light suddenly switched on. I could see things I had never seen before. I could see God trying to teach me a vital lesson. His love for me was palpable and overwhelming. I could also see how and why my teachers were trying to challenge and shape me, in addition to teaching me facts I needed to know. Suddenly, instead of anxiety, I was filled with awe and thanksgiving. God was "guarding my mind and heart" exactly as He said He would. The sweetest peace I have ever known filled my heart. **This was God sharing His life with me, giving me something that was His own.**

Which of His promises has God fulfilled in your life? What did He ask from you?

Do you make a point of noting God's promises as you read Scripture? So you will know what is available when you need it—along with God's conditions?

DOES GOD GIVE TO US IN RESPONSE TO OUR FAITH?

We hear that we should have "more faith" if we are to ask and receive from God. **But what is faith?** Is this some "inner condition of confidence that God will give us what we ask for"? Some say that a prayer was not answered because the praying person "did not have enough faith." Let me offer another viewpoint, one that dovetails with the words in Scripture, the structure of God's promises, and the principles of Covenant.

The word translated as "faith" and the word translated as "faithfulness" in the original Greek are the same word: *pisteo/pistis*. Whether "faith" or "faithfulness" is placed in the English text is purely at the discretion of the translator. Said another way, faith and faithfulness are two sides of the same coin—perhaps even the same side of the same coin. **If we replace the word faith with faithfulness in every verse, and vice versa, a new picture emerges**. We are in the habit of thinking of *faith*, generally, as an internal state of mind, or as the strength of our belief. We think of *faithfulness* as a specific and appropriate response.

Let us go back to the word *hesed*, the Hebrew word for God's love. This word refers to God's perfect inner life, from which flow His perfect actions and His perfect faithfulness to His Covenant with His people. Far more than simply "believing strongly that a particular outcome will occur," I believe that **faith refers to an inner life that first believes in Christ, and therefore affixes all hope for one's future to His Lordship, and therefore strives to increasingly follow His Lordship—which would translate into an increasingly faithful life.**

Beyond this, **the picture of *hesed* is to emulate the perfect inner life of God—from which flows His perfect love-in-action toward us.** That is, we must diligently, consistently strive to remove the inner imperfections from ourselves as these come to our attention. In Volume Two of this workbook series we will examine a step-by-step process to do this. Here, simply note: If we are confused about a matter, and our inner life reflects this confusion, we are to seek God's Word and will on this matter to clear up our confusion. Then we are to re-fashion our inner life according to His truth.

By this process—reading, studying, embracing, applying, and becoming the Word of God—we take on the attributes of Christ. We come to know His mind and heart. We increasingly come to know what He wants in a given situation, and we can pray according to His will. If our inner being is re-fashioned according to His will, we will live according to His will. I believe this to be the correct foundation for praying in faith. The words faith and faithful equally apply to the life we seek and the prayers we offer.

I believe this is a much better definition of the word "faith" versus the idea that we are to find some way to "strongly believe" that God will act as we desire (and not doubt that He will give us what we think we want).

What do you believe it means to pray "in faith"?

____

____

____

How can we develop more faith?

____

____

____

"And I will do whatever you ask in my name, so that the Father may be glorified ... "
JOHN 14:13

PRAYING IN JESUS' NAME

When we pray "in Jesus' name," what are we doing? Tacking on additional words, so God becomes more motivated to respond favorably? No. We are not to say, but to pray in a way that reflects the character, agenda, values, truth, and directives of Jesus.

"Whoever has My commands and keeps them is the one who loves Me. The one who loves me will be loved by my Father, and I will love them and show myself to them."
JOHN 14:21

One's name is synonymous with one's identity. We are to pray what Jesus would pray because of who He is. How do we know what He would pray? We must know Him. If we keep Jesus' commands (displaying our love for Him as we respond appropriately to His Lordship), He reveals Himself to us in special ways. The more we bring ourselves into alignment with Him, the more He reveals of Himself.

"If you remain in Me, and my words remain in you,
ask whatever you wish and it will be done for you."
JOHN 15:7

A LIFE OF FAITH

Such a life progressively incorporates Jesus' character, guidance system, and truth. That is: Christ is being formed in us. A "life of faith" means that one's inner qualities progressively align with the character of Christ, and one's behaviors increasingly align with the principles and practices within Covenant and God's Word.

Therefore, if we know, experience, apply, and are literally formed by God's Word, we can confidently ask for what we know Jesus would ask for. In addition, if we are living this life we are also having an ongoing, lively conversation with Him (since His Spirit is literally within us, and is always available for comment). Thus, He often gives us direct guidance and wisdom in situations that in turn inform our prayers.

Why would God only want to use His divine power to intervene in response to our prayers if we are praying what He would pray?

____

____

____

What do you think it would take to bring your mind, heart, and will into this kind of alignment with the life of God? Do you see this as a realistic objective?

____

____

____

How would you describe a life of faith?

____

____

____

Find one or more promises in Scripture for each item on the following page.

PARTAKING OF THE DIVINE NATURE (2 PETER 1:3-9)

God offers us:

His love, in the place of our hatred, malice, strife, and selfishness.

His righteousness, in the place of our unrighteousness.

His perfection and perfect obedience, in the place of our ignorance and sin.

His strength, in the place of our weakness and frailty.

His wisdom, in the place of our foolishness and misguided choices.

His truth, in the place of the blindness and deception that held/holds us captive.

His true riches, in the place of our material and spiritual poverty.

His glory, in the place of our humiliation and shame.

His joy, in the place of our discouragement, disillusionment, and despair.

His peace, in the place of our internal conflict, confusion, and anxiety.

His kindness, in the place of our harshness, contempt, and disdain.

His gentleness, in the place of our brutality, manipulation, and desire to dominate.

His faith, in the place of our doubt, insecurity, worry, and lack of faith.

His holiness, in the place of our uncleanness, rebellion, and evil desires.

His inheritance, as the only begotten Son of God, is now shared with those who were separated from the life of God and destined for eternal punishment.

The indestructible life of God is now within us, in place of the death (separation from God) that defined our previous earthly life—and would have defined our eternity.

These gifts—of new life and His life—are beyond anything we could ask or think.

Take a minute and consider the life God gives us, with all of its potential. Then consider the resources God provides for us to learn how to make the most of our new life: His presence (His Spirit) within us; His truth in the Scriptures; His Body, all of whom contain His presence, and all of whom join us on a similar journey. We are to build our new together-life. Covenant is His school of love and faithfulness.

This relationship is designed to produce within us, and from us, all that God requires. As if this is not enough, God offers to download His life into us.

See how great a love the Father has lavished on us, that we should be called children of God. And this is what we are.
I JOHN 3:1

We love because He first loved us.
I JOHN 4:19

In return for all of this, God asks for our love. How can we best respond? Let us consider God's love for us as shown through the remarkable, amazing, life-saving, life-giving gifts He has lavished on us. Is there anything not to like about God's gifts?! Instead, if we are enjoying this life more and more, our hearts will increasingly catch fire with passionate love for our Father in Heaven. If we are on His path—building the life He has given us, building the relationship we have with Him, increasingly enjoying the fruit of life-change—**how can we not wholeheartedly love our God?**

Let us take a closer look at the life God offers to bestow within our life. Consider each item on the list on the previous page. Consider what God's life looks like in each respect. Then, note all the aspects of our lives He offers to replace. Now consider your life in all of these respects. Consider what your life could look like if these aspects of your life mirrored God's life. Paint a picture in your mind and heart of the life you might have if God's life was lived through you. What specific elements of God's life would matter most to you? If His life became your life, what problems would this solve, what blessings would this produce, what relationships would this improve, what opportunities would this open up … and what would this life be like for you? Record your thoughts.

Now, examine each promise in Scripture that offers these needed and desired elements of God's life. What is required from you in order to receive each of these gifts of God's life? List these below, along with your plan to meet these requirements.

CHAPTER SEVEN

FALLING IN LOVE WITH GOD

We have talked about the underlying realities of Covenant, about God's call to us to engage in loving actions, and the imperative of faithfulness to God. What is God's desire? He wants us to love others deeply and well. He wants us to love Him and those He lives within. He wants us to love those who are created in His image. But God's point is ultimately not to tell us how to act. Why? Because **if we truly love someone, we do not need to be told how to act. We want to do the very things God instructs us to do**. So we return to this question: "What does it mean to love?"

True, our actions are important. A couple may be deeply in love at the altar. But what determines the quality of their relationship ten years into their marriage? How deep their feelings were at the outset, or how they have treated each other since they said, "I do"? Therefore, God calls us to conduct ourselves within Covenant in ways that build the best relationships. ***Love-in-action*** **builds** ***love-for-a-lifetime.***

Have you ever experienced a mismatch between the way someone says he or she feels toward you and the way they treat you? How did this impact you?

____

____

____

However, love is about more than how we act. Love is about our deepest feelings, hopes, and dreams. We want to be delighted in each other and excited to be with each other. We want admiration, respect, and appreciation to flow back and forth. We want to know and be known. We want to build together, explore together, and experience life together. We want our deepest passions to be unleashed within our relationship. **Love in its most pure form is a force that pulls all the parts of us together, and focuses their collective energies toward a single purpose—which is building** ***our together-life.***

This is the love God desires from us. It focuses and directs every fiber of our being, and impacts every moment of our existence—just as God intends Covenant to do. But this state of being does not simply descend upon us. We do not "fall in love" like falling into an unnoticed hole. The beginnings of love do well up from within us and flow back and forth between us. However, love-for-a-lifetime does not simply "occur." True love is not "found." It is not just about "finding the right person."

True love is built from the ground up. Our hearts, minds, and wills go through a series of steps and stages on the way to the fullness of this love. Why? **Because this is the way God created our minds, hearts, and wills to function** as we move toward giving our lives to each other, then as we learn to live *as one* in the ways God intends.

We do well to understand this process if we want to be deeply in love with God, for **we all must follow these same steps if we are to love Him in these ways.** Each step is a choice. We can move toward love within ourselves, or between two people. Or we can choose to move in the opposite direction.

If you have ever been deeply in love, review the steps in your journey.

____

____

____

Faithfulness within Covenant is about making the choice to love at every point—in the depths of our being and in the way we conduct ourselves. God realizes that we have much to learn about love. His Covenant plan equips us to love, gives us reasons to love, then teaches us how to love.

In your journeys of love, what were your strongest reasons to love, and what important lessons did you need to learn?

____

____

____

The journey of love includes many choices. We do not love perfectly at the outset because we have so many reasons to *not love*—questions, objections, competing agendas, misconceptions, wrong beliefs, and more. **Faithfulness within Covenant includes our responsibility to remove the impediments to love within ourselves.**

In your journey toward love, what factors moved you away from love? Did these prove to be an unnecessary distraction, or provide necessary protection?

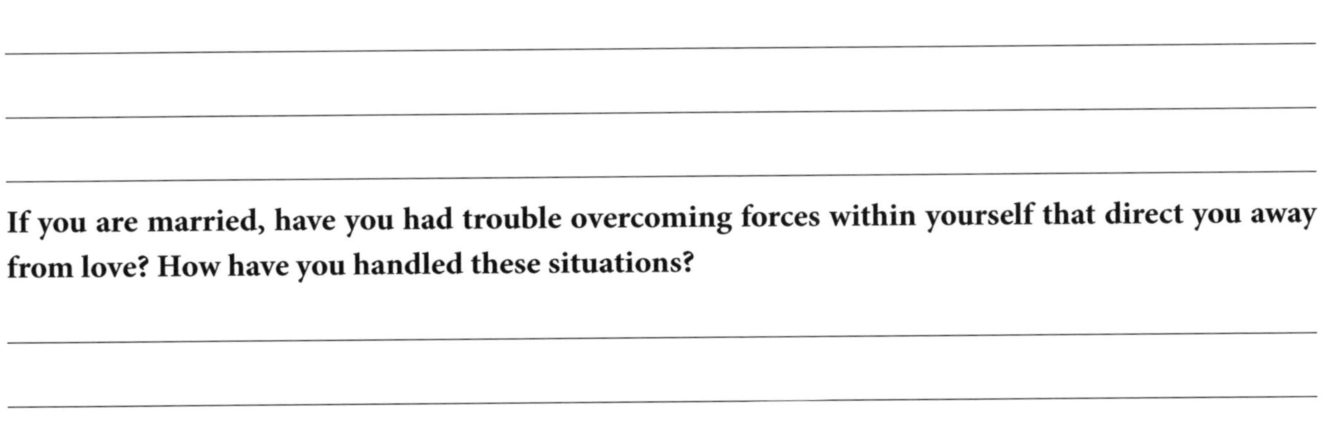

If you are married, have you had trouble overcoming forces within yourself that direct you away from love? How have you handled these situations?

THE PROCESS THAT BUILDS LOVE WITHIN US, AND BETWEEN US

I vividly remember the early months of my journey of love with the person who is now my wife. A conversation started that continues decades later. I wanted to know everything about her, and I still do. Our mutual interest and attraction caught fire. Delightful things happened within me—things I had never experienced. My mind, heart, and will were firmly focused on her—full of new thoughts, feelings, and determination. We began doing little things for each other, then larger things to bless each other.

Every thought I had about my future shifted … to our *future*—which was full of wonderful new possibilities. Holley rapidly became the most important priority in my life (other than God) as we built our relationship. Remarkable energy was available for this building process, which was conducted around my busy surgical practice, her career as a dental hygienist, and the needs of—between the two of us—seven children.

Most of what went on within me in the first few weeks was based on optimism about who I hoped she was, and the life I hoped we could build together. I asked these questions: is she a person who can love me, who does love me, and will love me? Is she a person worth loving, one who has the character to go the distance? Is she the kind of person I want to be joined to for the rest of my life? Can I entrust to her, not only my life, but the lives of my children?

This question was especially important, for both of us were previously married to people who proved to be anything but the people we thought they were when we wed. Both marriages ended prior to our meeting. In fact, it was the challenge of living with someone with a personality disorder (which led to seriously abusive behavior toward me and the children) that drove me to search out every detail of God's plan for marriage. I desperately sought God's answers in that situation. His gift, in the midst of the pain and heartache, was wisdom and understanding. God *does* have a plan, and it can work if His plan is lived out. But following His plan—faithfulness—remains a choice that both parties must make. Covenant is a mutual, all-in thing. Or, as in my case and Holley's, the other parties can choose to walk away.

As I considered our new relationship, I was keenly aware of the significance of one's *character*—and the significance of inconsistencies, the "little lapses" of integrity that can be telltale signs of serious character issues. I was also keenly aware that one person, no matter how hard he or she tries, cannot build a love-for-a-lifetime relationship on their own. It requires mutual hearts, approach, and effort.

This early ("I hope she is ... ") phase of any romance is replaced over time by what we experience. Over ensuing months, I found that my new friend wasn't who I thought she was. She was even better. She loves our Lord deeply. If she gave her word on a matter, I could count on her to follow through to the smallest detail. There was no subterfuge or manipulation. She was straightforward, honest, and transparent. She was unremittingly considerate, thoughtful, kind, and optimistic. She had a way of looking at the most difficult situations and seeing both opportunities and blessings.

So, *us* proved to be a good mixture. We had lots of fun and laughter. But we were also very good together when we faced challenges and had to solve problems (which seven children provide in unending supply). We had similar goals, values, and priorities. We both approached a romantic relationship with restraint that is squarely in line with God's plan. In addition, we could help each other grow spiritually. As we grew closer to the Lord, side by side, we grew closer to each other. We could combine our insights and search out deeper truths—about Scripture, circumstances, and the people around us. We developed a strong pattern of refining our approach to life based on Scripture.

Decades later, our communion, love, growth, and delight in each other continue ever stronger. Our relationship was, and is, consciously modeled on God's Covenant plan. This produced a marriage so good that we want to write books to help others build this kind of relationship—which, in fact, we have done.

Though our love at the outset was overwhelming, explosive, and consuming, we have learned so much more about true love over many years. Our love is still overwhelming, explosive, and consuming—only more so. Our love today is far more broad, deep, and intense than it was in those first months—which I still find difficult to believe. Our Covenant celebrations (which I will not describe further) continue to grow in intensity and meaning—for we have so much to celebrate. We have built a vast array of significant things together—but the most important thing we continue to build is each other. **Our lives have been radically transformed since we have known each other.** One truth stands out based on our experience: we only really learn how to love by being truly loved, and by truly loving—in ways that reflect God's definition of love.

Have you ever built a love-for-a-lifetime relationship? If not, why not?

___

___

___

If a previous relationship failed, given what we have learned about Covenant, what could each of you have done differently? What insight do human relationships offer about our heart toward God and our relationship with Him?

____

____

____

We love because He first loved us.
I John 4:19

A HEART OF LOVE IS BUILT BY A SERIES OF STEPS—EVEN LOVE FOR GOD

Have you ever considered falling in love with God? Do you know this is possible? When God asks us to love Him with our mind, heart, soul, and strength (Luke 10:27; Mark 12:30; Matthew 22:37), **do you realize that this is what He is asking us to do?**

True, there are some differences between spotting a person who attracts our interest, ultimately marrying, and building love-for-a-lifetime, versus the love relationship we can have with God. But there are fewer differences than we think. Both relationships begin with attraction and lead to entering a Covenant. The ever-deepening lifetime relationship God wants us to build within marriage **employs the same heart, mind, and will that we use to build a love relationship with Him.**

What does this process look like, and what are these steps? The following is only a brief outline, but a good starting point. Perhaps as we read through these steps, each of us can consider **how we might take these same steps in our walk with God.**

WE HAVE A CONNECTION

At times, we sense **a real connection** with someone. Our eyes meet, or there is a brief touch and we feel connected in some way. A mother and her child have a remarkably strong connection. We feel connected to our family—parents, siblings, aunts, uncles, cousins. We may feel connected with people with similar backgrounds, or people of the same racial, ethnic, or national origin. We say we "identify" with certain people because we share something important.

God designed Covenant to *create the strongest imaginable connection—and the strongest sense of connection*. Of course, we can actually be connected in some way, but fail to notice this reality. We may assign no special importance to our family members. The strongest relationships are *between those who are truly connected, who also recognize and deeply value* this reality.

Within a marriage, how connected are we? We are literally within each other. Our life is conjoined. What happens to one happens to the other. What foundation does this provide for our hearts toward each other? Do we recognize and appreciate this bond? **How do these realities of marriage promote love-for-a-lifetime?**

How connected are we to God? How does God intends this to impact our heart toward Him? Holley and I know of good families—people who have much to offer their family members—with children who simply wandered away as if these relationships meant nothing. In fact, there is an epidemic of alienation and isolation sweeping our nation. This is tragic. *How much more tragic if we do not recognize and properly respond to the connection that God offers us and accomplishes within us via Covenant?*

To be connected with a family full of wise, loving, successful people is truly wonderful. What is it like to be connected in a much deeper way with the living, loving God? If you have not deeply experienced this reality, take some time to do so. What is this experience like for you?

____

____

____

Before I formed you in the womb, I knew you.
JEREMIAH 1:5

"So, do not worry, saying, 'What shall we eat?' or 'What shall we drink?' or 'What shall we wear?' For the pagans run after all these things, and your heavenly Father knows that you need them. But seek first His Kingdom and His righteousness, and all these things will be given to you as well."
MATTHEW 6:31-33

"Indeed, the very hairs of your head are all numbered."
LUKE 12:7

For one standing next to a fire, if he does not appreciate the fire, it is as if he has no fire.
ANCIENT JAPANESE PROVERB

DO WE APPRECIATE BEING NOTICED BY GOD?

What happens when someone we admire in a romantic sense looks back at us with interest? Our hearts go nuts (if we are not already committed elsewhere). What happens when we read Scripture and *realize how much God is interested in us?* Is He someone we admire … or, if not, should we?

Beware of compartmentalizing God! When we hear things about Him, we may say, "Of course He is ________, He is God. He's perfect." Perhaps we think or feel nothing more. The old Japanese proverb quoted above contains a great truth: if we do not bother to notice and appreciate something, to us it is as if this thing does not even exist.

Do you ever marvel that the Creator of all things has personal encounters with you? Or that He orchestrated and executed a complex plan to re-create a state of oneness with you? Let all that God has done sink into your heart. How does it feel to be the object of such attention from your almighty, all-powerful Creator?

____

____

____

DO WE APPRECIATE WHO GOD IS?

The more we notice, learn, and appreciate something, **the more we value it**. I have found this to be true for vintage wristwatches, food, antiques, art, and many other things—especially my wife. Once she got my attention, I wanted to learn everything about her. *The more I learned, the more I appreciated her.* I learned even more, and appreciated her even more. If we see something as extremely valuable, we desire it in proportion to its value.

Many of us do not apprehend the reality of God. We view God as so different from us that we cannot relate to His feelings, or desires, or pain, or anger, or love. We may think life is "easy" for God—yet in His distress He sweated blood. Take a moment and ponder the decisions God has made on our behalf, and the perfect heart and mind behind His love. How does this make you feel toward Him?

____

____

____

DO WE UNDERSTAND WHAT GOD'S OFFER CAN MEAN FOR OUR LIVES?

We desire relationships, or things, largely based on how valuable we think these things will be for us. Satan has used this reality for millennia to lead people in wrong directions. How? By convincing us that some thing will be of great value to us … that is not. Instead, pursuing this thing will damage us and others. But once we embrace the idea of "the benefit," and our desire is kindled, other considerations fade from view.

Therefore, we need to be very careful about the things we view as "beneficial," then begin to desire. **Scripture terms Satan-inspired desires "evil desires."** These desires within us oppose God's plan. Given the relationship between our learning to appreciate something, and the formation of our desires, how do you think we could begin to desire the things God's desires for us?

Perhaps we should consider using our God-created internal mechanisms for their intended purpose: to produce a passion within us for God and the things of God. God is certainly perfection in every sense. Any relationship with Him, or notice by Him, or benefit offered from Him, would be of inestimable value. **But what about the amazing array of blessings and benefits He lavishes upon us within Covenant?** He gives us a new life re-made in His image; He lives within us; He gives us His truth as our guide for living; as well as giving us the in-the-moment leadership of His Spirit. He looks after our interests with as much enthusiasm as He looks after His own. **How valuable is the new life God offers us through our relationship with Him?**

Make a list of the ten most valuable things in your life, numbered in order of importance. Where does God, and your relationship with Him, land on this list?

____

____

____

To develop a passion for God, and our together-life, we must realize why our life in Christ is the most important aspect of our existence. God is the author of our life, and of life itself. How important would it be to learn how to live and love from Him?

____

____

____

Have we ever failed to notice the true value of something offered to us? I have a few really funny stories about missing "the chance of a lifetime." Don't we all? Here, we have the most important opportunity we will ever be offered. What should we do next?

At the same time, would it be good to reconsider the other things on our list—those that we also consider of great benefit? Would it be good to **clarify the relative importance of these things?** We only have so much time and energy. It would be a shame to affix our hopes for our best life to less beneficial things—and expend precious time and energy that could be better spent. Has our world deceived us about the true value of things—things that will prove to be of no real value?

"Where your treasure is, there your heart will be also."
MATTHEW 6:21

WHAT ARE WE INVESTING IN OUR RELATIONSHIP WITH GOD?

What do people do to build relationships? Many things can aid this process. We will consider a few. Please take the time to reflect on all you have learned about relationship-building, and enlarge this list for yourself! As we consider each item below, pay careful attention to the way in which *what we choose to do* impacts our mind, heart, and will. **For love to flow out of us, the proper foundation for love must be built within us.** When we choose to invest our best efforts (our treasure) in another's life, our heart toward this person predictably grows stronger.

We have spoken of the time, energy, and effort required to build our relationship with God. Everything in our life may be correctly viewed as *from* God, and for God. We are to sign up for His training process and make the most of every opportunity for growth. As we view this relationship, and such a training process on the front end, it may sound overly structured and confining. Something within us yearns for a bit more freedom, ease, and spontaneity in our relationships. Why can't we just "be ourselves," and be guided by what we want, and feel, and think? Why must we do *everything* God's way?

Consider why God desires all of this for us! He wants us to make *consistently constructive* decisions and build the deepest and most fruitful relationships. Why must we be trained, refined, and matured? To keep us from messing up our lives and relationships! Would you rather actually have a love-for-a-lifetime relationship on your fortieth anniversary, or remember "the good times you had" … as you sign the divorce papers? What is the difference? The difference is doing things *God's way instead of our way* … if these are different. **Is the real key to begin to desire for ourselves the same things God desires for us?**

What efforts are you currently making to build your relationship with God?

____

____

____

Is there any effort you would not make for God if He called upon you? Is He calling on you to do anything you have not yet done?

____

____

____

Let us fix our eyes on Jesus, the author and perfecter of our faith.
HEBREWS 12:2

SPENDING TIME TOGETHER: A JOY AND A NECESSITY

Once my relationship with Holley became something special, we both began clearing out less important things on our calendar. Why? Because the thing we most wanted to do was spend time with each other. We wanted more time to talk, to do things together, and to get to know each other. God is easier to access—since He is within us and all around us continuously. On the other hand, He can be more difficult to perceive than the person sitting next to me looking in my eyes. So, consider: **if you were offered an opportunity to spend some quality time with Jesus, would you clear your schedule?**

If you were offered an hour with Him, what would you do? If you had an hour a week, what would you do? If He made Himself available at any time, for as long as you like, **what are the most important things you could do together with Him?**

How much time do you spend with God, and how do you spend this time?

____

____

____

Set your minds on things above, not on earthly things.
For you died, and your life is now hidden with Christ in God.
COLOSSIANS 3:2, 3

DO WE NOTICE GOD … SOMETIMES, OFTEN, OR ALWAYS?

The above verse contains a crucial insight. We can direct our attention, focusing on one thing or another. We live in a dual existence. We inhabit the physical world. We navigate and understand this realm using our senses. But there is also another realm, a spiritual realm that we cannot perceive with our senses. Here, Jesus currently resides, along with angels and the spirits of departed humans. We also currently reside in this realm, within Jesus. **We cannot directly perceive things in the spiritual realm, but things from this realm may impact things in our physical realm in ways we can perceive—if we know what to look for.**

In fact, what is going on in our physical realm only makes sense when we realize that forces in the spiritual realm—that are "beyond the view" of our senses—have a massive impact on every human life. To understand these forces and their impact, we need God's revelation. Or we can turn to deceptive "explanations" from God's enemies.

HOW DO WE 'SET OUR MINDS ON THINGS ABOVE?'

Put your hand a foot or so in front of your face with your fingers spread. You can now focus on your fingers, or you can focus between your fingers at what is behind your hand. You have the ability to shift your focus back and forth between your fingers and what is behind them. Likewise, we can focus our attention on the day-to-day realties of our physical world, or we can focus on Jesus and the realities of the spiritual realm.

Problems arise if we focus solely on our physical world and its circumstances without taking into account Jesus and other spiritual realities. Unfortunately, we can ignore Jesus for hours, days, weeks, or longer, while our attention is riveted on this world. We can also ignore our husband or wife in the same way. What happens in either relationship if we do so?

Ideally, we remain aware of both realms—physical and spiritual—continuously. With practice, we can learn to focus both on our fingers and what is behind our hand. With practice, we can do something beyond checking in occasionally with Jesus, praying for a few minutes a day … or a week … or allowing Him to be out of our mind for days or weeks at a time.

Pray without ceasing.
I THESSALONIANS 5:17

What kind of practice allows us to do this? See the book *The Practice of the Presence of God* by Brother Lawrence (1614-1691). I did the simple things recommended in this book for several weeks during medical school. For the next forty-seven years I have literally had an *unending conversation with Jesus.* I am continuously aware of His presence, and I am keenly aware of the ways that spiritual forces affect people and circumstances around me.

What percentage of the time are you aware of only our physical realm, versus being also aware of the spiritual realm? How clearly do you see the impact of spiritual forces within our physical world? How can we train ourselves to be more aware of the totality of our existence—and of the God who created it all?

____

____

____

TIME AND ATTENTION … BUILDING HEARTS AND RELATIONSHIP

The bottom line is, while we are building a relationship we value, **we will want to spend time together.** The more benefit this relationship offers us, the more we will want to spend time together, and the more we will arrange our lives to allow this. **The best life is to do all of life together with God, moment by moment.** How do we pray in such a life? We can learn from books. But if we are conversing deeply with our most trusted friend, we simply talk about … anything and everything.

Do you have this kind of moment-by-moment interaction with God? If not, would you like to? How can you approach building this kind of relationship with God?

____

____

____

…we have not ceased praying for you and asking that you may be filled with the knowledge of His will in all spiritual wisdom and understanding, so that you will walk in a manner worthy of the Lord, to please Him in all respects, bearing fruit in every good work and increasing in the knowledge of God; strengthened with all power according to His glorious might, for the attaining of all perseverance and patience, joyously giving thanks to the Father.

COLOSSIANS 1:9-12

We proclaim Him, admonishing every person and teaching every person with all wisdom, so what we may present every person complete in Christ. For this purpose I also labor, striving according to His power which works mightily within me.

COLOSSIANS 1:28, 29

DOING THINGS FOR EACH OTHER

When Holley and I noticed each other in a romantic sense, we started trading kindnesses back and forth. We saw what worked and what did not. Over time, we learned more and more about each other's wants and needs. More and more over time, we did things that *really mattered for the other.*

This pattern turned into a friendly competition: who could out-bless the other. And it turned into a treasure hunt of sorts, as we searched for new things that mattered to each other. We found it truly more blessed to give, but also found it delightful to receive. What happened in our hearts as we gave and received in these ways?

What does God like? If you wanted to say "I love you" to God, what could you do? And what has He done lately that mattered to you? They say, "You can't out-give God." True—but it's fun to try! Simply consider all the things God asks for within Covenant, and the things He asks of us in Scripture. We all have a "love language." **Obedience is God's love language (John chapter 14)**. The above Scriptures contain a number of items that please God. We can choose one item after another and find a way to give God this gift. Then, watch what happens next, inside us and between us.

"Inasmuch as you do something for the least of these, you do it for Me."
MATTHEW 25:40

God's love language is also Covenant. We speak His language by loving those in His church body. Also, since Jesus is within every believer, when we do loving things for our brothers or sisters, we are actually doing these things for Him.

The most important difference between our new self and our old self is this: our new self can please God. Would it be good to devote ourselves to doing so? We can start by making a list of ways we can make Him smile ... and leave ourselves smiling as well. Start your list here. :-))

____

____

____

In everything give thanks; for this is the will of God for you in Christ Jesus.
I THESSALONIANS 5:18 (NASB)

I have learned the secret of being content in any and every situation.
PHILIPPIANS 4:12

NOTING AND APPRECIATING THE EFFORTS OF ANOTHER

As we make a serious effort to build a relationship with God, He takes delight in doing special things for us. There have been countless times in my life when unexpected and delightful things just "showed up," when things turned out unexpectedly well, or something turned out to be surprisingly beneficial. This pattern goes far beyond mere coincidence, good luck, or random occurrences. **This is the hand of God offering blessings in response to our faithfulness, and to a heart that desires to know Him.**

God is always active in all of our lives, and in many more ways than we can perceive. However, we may not recognize what He is doing. Or, even if we do notice, we may under-appreciate what God is doing for us.

Have you ever made a considerable effort to do something for someone ... and they barely noticed? Or they criticized the gift, or were in some other way dismissive? How did this feel? And how did it impact your relationship? (Perhaps: "Never again will I ___ !") **Have we ever responded this way to God?** How do we think God reacts to us if we fail to notice or appreciate His love-in-action toward us?

How often do we find serious fault with our life circumstances, or with everyone around us? Have we ever considered that **everything God ordains or allows in our life is His perfect gift for us?** We all know what we want. But **how many of us know what we really need ... except God?** Do we genuinely trust in God? Do we appreciate His love in every situation—even if He is trying to refine us through adversity?

If we are trying to build a relationship, a great move is to notice and appreciate the efforts of the other person—and the heart behind these efforts, even if a gift is not quite what we expect or want. (This is far more true if the gift is actually perfect!)

Why does God instruct us to "give thanks in every situation"? How might He be blessing us through this instruction?

____

____

____

Would you prefer being "content in every situation," or continually upset by life ("I am simply not going to settle for ... ")? How did Paul achieve this state of contentment regardless of his circumstances? What do you think he saw and appreciated as he considered the role God played in his life?

____

____

____

And without faith it is impossible to please Him, for whoever would draw near to God must believe that He exists, and that He rewards those who seek Him.
HEBREWS 11:6 (ESV)

LEARNING THAT WE ARE BETTER TOGETHER

We must realize from experience that *us*—God and I—are really good together (if I actually follow His lead). **God wants us to enjoy Him**. Made in His image, we are capable of laughter—because He laughs. Without question, we offer Him a wealth of reasons to laugh. The world He created and the life He gives us offer many reasons to smile. But these gifts pale in comparison to being with Him as we navigate this life.

God has in mind the best goals, values, and priorities for our life. We have only to bring ourselves in line with His plan. God's leadership produces spiritual growth and maturity. As we grow to be more like Him, and see the benefits and blessings of doing so, we grow closer to Him. His deeper insights and truths lead to more balance, peace, and wisdom. We can refine our approach to life in every way based on Scripture. As we walk with Him, His love is poured into us in a growing array of ways.

As we experience these benefits, how are our thoughts and feelings about God impacted? How is our willingness to devote ourselves to Him and His path impacted? Over time, we realize that **the only future worth having flows from our together-life.**

What is required if we are to experience the blessings of our together-life? Our lives must change for the better. If we remain stuck in our "old life," experiencing few, if any, changes, what is there to enjoy, appreciate, and value about our relationship with God? Is it fair to say that the extent to which our together-life yields benefits depends—not on God—but on our degree of faithfulness to Him? If so, what is the path to deeply valuing our together-life with God?

____

____

____

Since you have been raised with Christ, set your heart on things above,
where Christ is, seated at the right hand of God.
COLOSSIANS 3:1

SEE A FUTURE FULL OF NEW POSSIBILITIES IN OUR TOGETHER-LIFE

God gives us a totally transformed self and offers us a radically transformed life. When the possibility of a together-life with a wonderful person dawned on me, I spent a lot of time dreaming about what this new life could be—and how we would get there. We are offered a together-life with a perfect God. This is vastly more wonderful.

How much time do we spend thinking about God's involvement in our lives beyond helping us out of our current difficulties? How much time do we devote to understanding God's offer, what He has already done within us, and what this can mean for us if we make the most of His offer?

Such a vision for our life is not wishful thinking—if we follow God's plan. **Time spent developing a new vision for our life is a vital part of redirecting our lives—from our old life to our new life.**

Given the changes God has worked within us and the resources He makes available to us, what changes do you see as possible and desirable in your life?

____

____

____

God causes all things to work together for good for those who love God,
for those who are called according to His purposes.
ROMANS 8:28 (NASB)

In fact, the life we really want is not even the life we want. Instead, it is the life God wants for us! We can confidently affix our desires, hopes, and dreams to Him and His plan for our lives, knowing that if our life does not turn out the way we envision, it is because God has an even better plan for our lives. After forty-seven years I can say this with 100 percent confidence.

Given the changes God has worked within us and the resources He makes available to us, what changes do you think God wants to see in your life?

____

____

____

I consider that our present sufferings are not worth comparing with the
glory that will be revealed in us … the freedom and glory of the children of God.
ROMANS 8:18, 21

BUT WAIT! THERE'S MORE …

On this earth we get only a taste of what is to come in our together-life with God. My dreams of a together-life with Holley came true. Our life has been delightful for decades. Is our eternal life with God going to be incomparably better? I love the glimpses of eternal life we get from those who have near-death experiences. How often do we delight ourselves by considering what *this eternal life will be like for us?*

How do you envision the experience of an eternal life in God's presence?

WELCOMING GOD INTO EVERY PART OF OUR LIVES

This may sound a bit redundant, since God inhabits the core of our being and fills all of creation—including us. Regardless, through a series of decisions, we must *welcome Him* into every aspect of our life. We agree to do this in principle when we enter the New Covenant, as we do in a marriage. But, as in marriage, the actual functional merger of lives is a process.

Are there places inside of us we want God to stay away from? If so, why? Are there things He will take exception to … that we still value more than Him? Are we ashamed of something, or frightened by what may be deep within us? Are we struggling with something we are afraid to reveal to Him, when instead we need to seek His help? Are we afraid God would not love us if He really knew—as if He doesn't? If we have learned that we are better together in some ways, will we not be better together in all ways? God will prove this if we simply invite Him in everywhere and watch what happens next.

Remember, within Covenant there is no protected "personal" space. Why? Because the things we would try to hide are the very things that will stand in the way of our "oneness" in marriage, or of our maturity and Christlikeness within the New Covenant. Consider the things you least want God to know about you … then consider how to bring these things before Him and begin to deal with them. What are these things?

"Do not let your hearts be troubled. You believe in God. Believe also in Me."
JOHN 14:1

TRUSTING AND TRUSTING IN GOD

These are the criteria for entering Covenant with God. But it is vital for us to examine our lives, to see **how much we actually trust God**, and then trust in Him in actual practice. We humans have a remarkable capacity for saying we believe something, but not necessarily *living as if we do.*

Trust in God does not occur in a vacuum—as simply "I do" or "I don't." Instead, there is a crucial equation here: do I trust God with my life absolutely, in every way, and live accordingly? Or do I trust God … to a point in some situations, but in other situations I trust my own perception or follow the world's approach?

When we consider what it would be like to devote every part of our self and life to God, are we excited by this prospect? Or do we cringe a bit? If so, why?

____

____

____

The real question is: "What do I trust more than God, and why?" There has been a massive effort in our lifetime to replace God's Word as the source of absolute truth with other sources: "my truth," science, the opinions of "experts," cultural trends, and more.

We have an enemy whose most important priority is to keep us from following God's plan and enjoying the blessings of this plan. He does this in our lives in the same way he did with Adam and Eve: **by causing us to doubt God's approach.**

We often do not recognize the source of our questions about God. Notice that we don't need to be convinced that God is wrong to refrain from following Him. We just need to have unanswered questions, or not be totally sure about God, to turn from His guidance to other sources. Thus, it is vital to identify and answer any lingering questions about the truth of God's Word, or lingering question about Him.

MY PERSONAL JOURNEY AND STRUGGLE

I came from a more skeptical starting point than most. I had a lot of questions about God and the truth of His Word. As I considered giving my life to God, these unanswered questions were the obstacle to accepting His offer.

I identified my key questions and started to search for answers. To my surprise, I found highly credible answers to each question, and to a few other important questions that had not occurred to me. **God has gone to great lengths to provide a compelling body of evidence to prove the source and truth of His Word.** My questions about God, when written down, simply reflected confusion and ignorance on my part. I had no actual evidence to refute God's claims … because no such evidence exists.

What lingering questions do you have about God: His Word and its credibility, His love for us, or His willingness to display His love in our lives?

____

____

____

HOW DO WE KNOW WHETHER WE TRULY TRUST IN GOD?

The practical question comes down to this: if God says something is true, or needed from us—and our perceptions or our previously embraced beliefs differ from God's Word—what do we do? What source do we deem most credible? Do we *believe in ourselves*, other people, our world, or God? Our real answer is revealed by whose word we choose to follow. For over forty years I have never regretted obeying God.

When God's Word says one thing, but you think you should do something else, what happens next? Does this answer the question, "Who do I believe in?"

____

____

____

Whether or not we truly believe in God will impact how we feel. If we trust someone with our lives and believe them to be totally credible, we feel one way about them. If we aren't sure how much we can really trust someone, how do we feel—even if we have no reason of substance to doubt this person?

God's Word and His character have stood up under the closest scrutiny by the harshest skeptics for millennia. He has already answered any questions any of us might have. He doesn't mind you asking **if you are willing to honestly consider His answer.**

But there is another element to trust: experience. We do well to extend our trust to God. He will reward this trust by proving His faithfulness toward us in myriad ways … if we follow Him—which we will refrain from doing if we do not totally trust Him.

When have you trusted God in the face of conflicting advice, perceptions, or feelings? What happened next?

____

____

____

This is why I love my wife far more today than I did decades ago, when we began our relationship. Based on preliminary evidence, **it seemed that I could trust her, so I decided to do so.** Then, by experience, I found that I could trust her more than any person I have ever known. I chose to trust her, then found from experience why I could and should trust her.

Based on this experience, **I began to trust in her.** Beyond the factual accuracy of her words, I became convinced that **her deepest desire was for my benefit,** and that **her character would consistently live out this desire.** When I asked her to marry me, I was as sure as I could be that I could safely entrust my heart and future to her. After decades of experience, I learned that my confidence was well placed. How has this experience impacted my heart toward her?

To the faithful you show yourself faithful ...
PSALM 18:25

Is Holley perfect? No. Is her love perfect? Not quite. Is she God? No. However, He is within her and often communicates to me through her. Do I have far more reasons and far more experiences that support *trusting* and *trusting in* God? Absolutely. What impact has my experience had on my heart toward God? What about yours?

How has your heart been impacted by God's love and faithfulness?

____

____

____

Endure hardship as discipline; God is treating you as His children.
For what children are not disciplined by their father?
HEBREWS 12:7

Consider it all joy, my brothers and sisters, when you encounter various trials, knowing that the testing of your faith produces endurance. And let endurance have its perfect result, that you may be perfect and complete, lacking in nothing.
JAMES 1:2-4 (NASB)

...even though now for a little while you have been distressed by various trials, so that the proof of your faith, being more precious than gold, which perishes though tested by fire, may be found to result in praise, glory, and honor at the revelation of Jesus Christ.
1 PETER 1: 6, 7 (NASB)

GOD LOVES US IN MANY WAYS—AND SOME WAYS WILL BE UNPLEASANT

The extent to which we trust in God will be tested. How? By unpleasant circumstances that God allows in our lives. Does God not notice or care about our well-being, and the well-being of those we care about? Or, is God allowing such things for their long-term benefit in our lives and the lives of others—despite the way things look from our vantage point? **How much do we really trust in God?**

If you have children and are a good parent, you know there are times your child does not like you. Why? Because you compel them to do things they do not want to do in order to teach them important lessons. A wise child, over time, realizes that the best life is found by following the directions of someone more wise than themselves.

Our children came back in their twenties and thanked us profusely for teaching them many of the lessons they deeply disliked learning in their childhood and teenage years.

God instructs us at many points to "give thanks." In part this is for His benefit, but perhaps even more, it is for our benefit. Why? **We often take God and all that He does for granted, as if an outpouring of blessings is how our lives are supposed to be.** We may become angry at God if the flow of blessings in our life stops, even if the reason is us. God wants us to recognize that our choices matter. His heart desires even better things for us than the things He withholds. If we do not realize this—and adjust—we may be faced with scenarios that we find even more difficult to understand.

We may know God expects and requires much from us. We may know His blessings are contingent on our faithfulness. We may pour everything we have into pleasing God, **yet our life still falls apart.** Or we suffer a major loss despite fervent prayers. Has God stopped loving and caring? Does He not notice what is happening to us, or to someone we care about? A great verse to review on this point: Romans 5:3-5.

The truth is this: we put our lives in God's hands to do with as He pleases. He ultimately desires the best for us. But we may have a lot to learn about life, ourselves, and Him along the way. Some life lessons can only be learned through pain and suffering. We did not sign up for an easy life; we offered our lives to God to live our best possible life.

Though He was God's Son, He learned obedience through what He suffered.
HEBREWS 5:8 (HCSB)

Let us fix our eyes on Jesus, the author and perfecter of our faith, who for the joy set before Him endured the cross, despising its shame, and is seated at the right hand of the throne of God.
HEBREWS 12:2 (ESV)

Oddly—and perhaps in sharp contrast with our thoughts—our best life can only be found by stripping away valued things in our life *that we rely upon too much*. God may strip away everything else in our life that we value to show us that He is enough … period. And He is. Paul refers to this lesson in Philippians 4:12. (See II Corinthians chapter 4 for a more in-depth discussion of this point, especially verses 17 and 18.)

… but He disciplines us for our good, so that we may share in His holiness. For the moment, all discipline seems not to be pleasant, but painful; yet, to those who have been trained by it, afterward it yields the peaceful fruit of righteousness.
Hebrews 12:10, 11 (NASB)

In what we think is our darkest hour, we can always give thanks for what God is doing in our lives—even if we do not understand His long-term plan in the moment. God uses all things as part of our training process, both pleasant and unpleasant. Instead of, "Why me?" we can ask, "What are You trying to teach me?" If we are trying to say "I love you" to God, this response may be near the top of His list.

If we think *this is truly our darkest hour*, consider what our life would be if we were eternally separated from Him? That moment of judgment would, in reality, be anyone's darkest hour. Instead, God is blessing us in His perfect way, one that in the end will be most beneficial for us. For the coming peaceful fruit, we can be grateful. We can be even more grateful for a God who cares enough to do what is necessary to help us build our best possible life.

As we begin our new life in Christ, we have questions, hopes, dreams, fears, and conflicting thoughts and emotions. We have much to learn about our new life, and we must build this life from the ground up. What have you learned about God and your new life from experience since starting your journey?

___

___

___

___

___

___

___

___

___

CHAPTER EIGHT

EMPLOYING AND ENJOYING GOD'S GREATEST GIFT

GOD'S MOST PRECIOUS GIFT IS *OUR NEW LIFE*

Our life is an expression of God's love in several ways. Our flesh and blood bodies came into being through an act of love—the sharing of life between two people. By this act the two either became *one flesh* or celebrated their entry into a one-flesh relationship. Through this act, a new human life came into being. Then, when we enter the New Covenant, and are born again He creates a new life within us, one that is in harmony with Him. He also receives our life within Himself and places His life within us.

As an act of love, God gave a set of rules and principles for living to the Jewish people—the "Law of Moses." These rules directed people to act in the most constructive ways (Matthew 22:40). The Israelites were to worship and serve God only. God forbade His people to worship the gods of other nations or follow their practices. Why? Because these gods—as agents of the kingdom of darkness—instructed their worshippers to live in ways that harmed themselves and others. God insisted that the Israelites protect themselves from this influence so His people could build the best lives and the most constructive society.

However, due to the "nature problem" in His own people (and all of humanity), the phrase "inconsistent at best" describes Israel's faithfulness to their God. They frequently turned to the gods of surrounding countries and followed their rebellious directives for living (I Corinthians 10:20). They returned to God only when the consequences of their rebellion—and the resulting withdrawal of God's blessings and protection—ravaged their lives and their nation.

Even when people strictly obeyed God's laws (in response to seeing Jerusalem and the rest of Israel obliterated for their unfaithfulness, first by the Assyrians, then the Babylonians), they often did so for wrong reasons (e.g., the Pharisees). Though they were God's chosen people, the Jews refrained from wholeheartedly choosing God and returning His love.

Why? For two related reasons: First, their "nature problem" caused them to innately resist God and gravitate toward the voice of His enemy (the fallen angels worshipped by other nations). The second reason was the character and way of life that people came to desire, then chose to build their lives upon. Throughout the ancient world, and within Israel, people's lives and society were deeply influenced by Satan's most fundamental lie. That is: "We end up with a better life if we follow Satan's guidance instead of God's 'restrictive' rules." God, after all, limits our "sexual expression." He directs us to display honesty and integrity, to care for those around us, and to pursue justice. He "confines" us to our best life so we do not ill-use or brutalize our neighbors.

Sadly, many people in ancient Israel found it easier to lie, steal, and manipulate their way to their ideal of the "good life," just as we do today. When faced with the consequences of their behavior and the uncertainties of life, the Israelites offered gifts and sacrifices to foreign gods to enlist their favor—including at times sacrificing their own children. When this approach to the issues of life failed, some turned back to God—at least temporarily.

Oddly, these same behaviors surround us today … for the same reasons. Is it a coincidence that our "cultural trends" point us toward the same behaviors commended by the "other gods," the ones the real God warned us to avoid?

Ultimately, God sent His Son to earth to offer a New Covenant with Himself. He devised a relationship that offered everything needed by every person, Jew or Gentile: a new nature, forgiveness for sins, and a restored oneness with their Creator. Humanity, in Covenant with God, would be washed clean. They would no longer be slaves to sin.

The new life promised in the Gospel is like opening that long-awaited Christmas present we so much want to use and enjoy. But when we open the box we find a pile of parts and instructions written in a difficult-to-understand language. We want to employ and enjoy this gift, but "some assembly is required." We stare at what is in front of us, not sure where to start. How do we make the most of God's gift, this new life?

HOW DO WE BEGIN BUILDING OUR NEW LIFE IN CHRIST?

In one sense *we already have a new life*. But in another sense, *we just began a lifelong journey toward building the life of Christ within ourselves.*

One common experience among Christians is a **new sense of peace** in the core of our being. Why is this? Our true self was formerly separated from God and opposed to Him. Now our new true self is in harmony with God and joined to Him. Our own war with God, waged from the core of our being, is over. We are at peace with our Creator.

We have a **new desire to please God.** We suddenly care what He thinks and what He wants for us. This is coupled with a new desire to read His Word, and new understanding when we do so (I Corinthians 2:12). His Spirit within us (the "Spirit of Revelation," Ephesians 1:17) begins to progressively open our eyes to understand the truths in His Word and to see things within ourselves that are not in harmony with Him (John 16:8).

We sense the reality and presence of God. We begin a conversation with Him. We sense that He has a new plan for our lives—within Scripture—and His plan within Covenant that we are unfolding in this workbook series. We begin implementing the truths we learn from God's Word in our lives, and we enjoy the blessings of doing so. We begin to understand God's larger plan for us, on earth and in eternity. We grapple with the concept of Jesus' Lordship versus what we want and what we do. In sum, we find ourselves having new goals and desires, making new decisions, and experiencing new challenges.

What changes did you note in your new life—immediately, then over time?

____

____

____

We have a new family—the Body of Christ. We often note a new affinity toward these people. To engage with our new family, we typically join a local church. A strong, biblically based church is an important part of God's plan for us. Unfortunately, in our current Christian culture, many focus on local church activities as if these are the sum of God's plan for us. Also, some have had negative experiences in churches, and they are motivated to not repeat these experiences. How do we keep all of this in perspective?

For each of us, a Covenant relationship exists with every member of the Body of Christ. **A local church body should be a place where we learn to fulfill the obligations and responsibilities inherent in this relationship.** The focus should not be solely on our local group. Instead, we should have in view the entire Body of Christ. A local church should be the place where we are on the receiving end of Jesus' New Command, experiencing His love poured out within His Body. At the same time, we should be building a heart of love for His Body as we serve, give, and do life with each other.

However, many today—including pastors and teachers—do not seem to understand the nature of our relationship with God, or with each other, or understand God's definition of love and the training process necessary to display His love. It would be a great service to the Body of Christ for those who do understand such things to teach them to our brothers and sisters.

"I have come in my Father's name, and you do not accept Me; but if someone else comes in his own name, you will accept him. How can you believe, since you accept glory from one another but do not seek the glory that comes from the only God?"
John 5:43, 44

If God's Word is not honored as His Word, whose ideas and plan will lead, guide, and form people? If God's plan is not lived out, churches do not function as intended. If God's plan is not lived out, our progress toward Christlikeness is hindered. Thus, it is very important to **find a church body that is guided by His Word and His plan, a body that is truly under the Lordship of Christ.**

At the same time, **no group or person will be a perfect representation of Christ's life**, and we should not expect this. God receives us "as we are." But His intent is not to leave us as we are. **We must remember that we are all somewhere on the path to Christlikeness.** This applies equally to everyone who leads or attends any church, and to ourselves. God's intends that we encourage and help each other on our respective journeys. Within Covenant, regardless of another's understanding or practices, **we are to display God's love and acceptance, and have a gracious and redemptive attitude toward them.** For those who are not within the Body, we are still to be gracious and kind.

Frankly, at times it will be impossible to view a person and discern which of these is the case, due to people's inconsistent choices. This is appropriate, because it is not our role to make this determination. We are not to render judgement about another's spiritual state or their behavior. Instead, our role is simply to speak God's truth in love when this is appropriate.

Blessed is the person who does not follow the advice of wicked people,
take the path of sinners, or join the company of mockers.
Psalm 1:1

We are to employ discernment, though, about whom we join with, and walk together with, on our journey. It is important to find people who are actually drawing closer to God, and join together with them on their journey. We need to hear strong Biblical teaching. We need to begin serving the needs of others in the Body of Christ and our community. We need to gather in small groups to build deeper friendships, and to learn and apply Scripture together.

However, in light of God's plan—to build a deep and intimate relationship with Him that produces radical transformation in our lives—**we must keep a larger picture in mind.** Does any local church's "few-hours-of-activity-a-week" plan accomplish all of God's purposes? Would devoting all of our time to these same activities accomplish God's purposes? **If not, what is needed to produce the kinds of changes God intends?**

What plan would be needed to build your new life in Christ to maturity?

____

____

____

GROWING AND BEARING FRUIT REQUIRES A PROPER ROOT SYSTEM

When we see a large, beautiful, fruitful tree, we only see the tree and its fruit. **What do we not see? The root system that allows what we do see to exist!** Now, suppose we see someone whose life aligns in many ways with Christ's life. We may admire their life and its impact. As in the case of the tree, though, what do we not see?

If our new life in Christ is to grow into something large, strong, and fruitful, we must build its root system. **This root system is our inner life, our private life with God.** This includes Scripture study, meditation, and application; prayers and conversation with God; the insights and instructions we receive from His Spirit; and simply time spent in His presence, worshipping Him. **This is the heart of our training process. But these things are unfamiliar to us. We will not know how to do any of this.**

Therefore, we need one more thing: we need each other in a special way. Anyone who is living an increasingly Christlike life will be doing what is necessary to produce such a life. We only see these inner parts of another's life if they choose to reveal them to us. **This is a key aspect of mentoring: the process in which a mature Christian spends time imparting his or her inner life to a younger believer.** Spending one-on-one time with a more mature believer is perhaps the most important single element of God's plan for our growth and development. **Yet, in our current culture, few recognize the need to mentor others, or to be mentored.**

When my journey with God began in 1977, I became part of a local church and another ministry (the Navigators), both of which emphasized such one-on-one involvement. Ever since, I have sought out mature believers, and learned from them. I am always open to spending time with younger believers, and have done so on many occasions through the years. This book series draws heavily from these mentoring experiences.

I have watched God's plan work in amazing ways in many lives—if we carry out His plan. I have watched others not follow God's plan, not change, and not grow. I have spent years trying to understand why a person chooses one or the other.

WE HAVE A NEW IDEAL FOR OUR LIFE: THE LIFE OF CHRIST

God did not just offer us instructions from behind His desk in Heaven. Christ fully entered into our human life. The righteousness, holiness, and *hesed* of God were on full display before a watching and often hostile audience in the midst of our world. **Christ's perfect life is our ideal for life in the midst of our circumstances.**

In the end, God most rewards those who overcome (Romans 12:21; Revelation 2:7, 17, 26; 3:21; 21:7). But overcome what? He wants us to overcome any obstacle on our journey toward Him and the life He intends for us. The most important battle we all must win, therefore, is the battle we are about to describe—the battle that takes place within ourselves.

OVERCOMING OUR RESISTANCE TO GOD AND HIS PLAN

WHY DO WE STILL STRUGGLE TO OBEY GOD?

We now can choose to obey at any and every point. We can make every choice in a way that pleases God. But we can also make choices that violate His will, heart, plan, and Word. All of us predictably choose to do the latter with some frequency. So two vital questions remain:

- Why do our choices not consistently align with God?
- What is God's plan to change us and our lives beyond what He has already done upon our entry into Covenant?

YOU ARE HERE ...

If we have a map, and we have a destination in mind, what else must we have for our map to be of any value? We must know where we are now. So **let us first look at our current life, and how this life came to be.** Only then will God's roadmap for change make sense.

HOW DO WE CHOOSE WHAT WE DO?

First, let's consider what goes on inside us as we make choices. When we "go back and forth" about an issue, we are hearing different ideas coming from different sources within us. One idea may come from our experience, another from the advice or example of others, another may come from God's Word or God's Spirit. Our personal beliefs, feelings, values, and desires come into play. **"Making a decision"** means we choose the inner voice we trust most and implement the idea this voice recommends.

So, our real choice is which source we choose to trust. The curious thing is why our first and only move is not to simply trust God's Word above any other, given who God is and our stated intention to make Him our Lord. Still, often we do not.

We often make choices without making choices … in the moment. Many of our daily decisions to do, say, think, feel, value, or seek come from *habits.* We simply "do what we have always done," because at some point we chose this path. It worked well enough, and we continue to live out the same pattern.

We can now make choices that align with God. But a lot must happen before we know what God wants in a particular situation. Then, before we decide to do as He says. Then, before we go from intention to action—which may include becoming able to do or be as He instructs. **All of this must occur, and more, before we faithfully and consistently follow God's instructions.**

Think back to a time when you struggled to obey God. What was going on in your mind and heart? What happened next? How did your decision turn out?

____

____

____

We built our old life, for the most part, because we wanted to live in these ways. We have our habits, our comfort zone, and our accustomed things. We have our familiar practices, approaches, strategies, values, and desires. We have our viewpoint and our beliefs. We devote ourselves to living these things out. Doing what we have always done, our lives generally held together well. Even the unpleasant aspects of our life are familiar. For the most part, we cope with them well enough.

We do want God to change some things about our lives. Beyond this, though, we are fine with things the way they are. When life works fairly well from our perspective, at least in the short term, there are several hurdles to life-change—even when the One telling us to change is God.

Consider the difference between what you want to change about your life and the changes God wants to see. What do you feel when you consider this discrepancy? Excitement … fear … or what? Why do you feel this way?

____

____

____

As a Christian, we have a new desire to please God—sometimes. As we learn His Word and ways, we make different choices. But most of us are still busy building and living "our life." **From our perspective, it may be unclear how God and His desires fit into my life.** How much effort should we devote to God's considerations when we have so many considerations of our own? And, in a given situation, are His ideas really better?

If we think this way—and we all do—**to what life are we now devoting ourselves? Our old life?** The one God tells us to "take off" as we "put on" our new life? So **our first journey, beginning with our first breath in our new life, is to begin to understand—and care—what God thinks about "our old life," and why.** After all, we did vow to make Him our Lord.

How does the Covenant reality of "our life" versus "my life" matter here?

____

____

____

HOW DOES GOD HELP US WANT TO DO WHAT IS TRULY BEST FOR US?

To fully understand God's plan for our new life, we must understand more about another gift He has given us: **how God created our mind, heart, and will. He designed the ways these work together to create our lives.** If we understand our inner workings, it will help us to carry out God's plan.

Here is the question: "Why do we want to do something?" What are your thoughts?

____

____

____

GOD CREATED THREE POWERS WITHIN US

Within us, God created three separate realms—our mind, heart, and will. These three aspects of our *self* work together to construct our life. We can better understand how these function if we consider them to be **three powers that He placed within us.** Just as with our physical powers, these three can be strengthened through exercise, and trained to function at a very high level. Or, they may remain weak, work in a random fashion, and function together poorly.

We will term these three powers *the power of assent or dissent; the power of attention;* and *the power of intention.* These powers are described in detail in *The New Covenant.* Here, let's look at each briefly.

THE POWER OF ASSENT AND DISSENT

We are each given the prerogative of deciding for ourselves what we believe to be true, right, real, or beneficial—or the opposite. That is, **we can agree with, or disagree with, any given idea.** No one can make us believe something if we choose not to do so. We may carefully consider an idea, research it, study it—or merely accept something we are told, or that is implied. We also draw conclusions about *how things really are* from personal experience.

Whatever the path, **there is a point when we render our decision about an idea**. If we agree with this idea, something very important and powerful happens. This idea shifts from being *an idea,* to becoming *our idea.* We just welcomed this idea within ourselves, and embraced this idea as one of our beliefs, as a part of *our truth.* We are all familiar with this process. What may escape our attention, though, are the other things that occur within ourselves as a result of our decision to embrace an idea.

Would you agree or disagree that our choice of *what to believe* or *disbelieve* is one of our most important choices? Why, or why not?

____

____

____

THE POWER OF ATTENTION

This is a broad and multifaceted power. Our "heart" is usually associated only with emotions, but this realm involves far more than our feelings. At its most simple, it is our ability to focus our attention on one thing or another. If we hold a hand a foot in front of our face with fingers spread, we can choose to focus on our fingers, or focus on what is behind our hand. We can direct our focus back and forth. *In the same way, we can choose to focus on one thought or another, one feeling or another, one goal or another.*

Another aspect of this power is *valuing one thing versus another.* We tend to focus more attention, time, and resources on things we deem to be more important, and less attention or no attention on things we deem to be less important.

Inherent in this power is our emotional response. We feel positive emotions toward things we deem to be true, right, real, and beneficial, and negative feelings toward ideas we reject. The more important we deem something to be, the stronger our feelings will be in either direction.

Our belief in potential benefit plus our emotional response form the foundation for our *desires.* The strength of our desire is in proportion to how important we deem something to be. This Power of

Attention, in sum, provides us with our likes, dislikes, desires, preferences, values, and priorities, along with the general sense of importance we assign to any particular thing.

List all the ways you use this power each day to determine the relative value of things, and direct your attention toward, or away from, certain things.

THE POWER OF INTENTION

Something may be true, real, right, or beneficial—and important for us. The next step is to use our power of intention to decide **what, if anything, we are going to do about this issue. And, how committed are we to this end?** How much adversity are we willing to overcome, and how much sacrifice are we willing to make to see this thing accomplished? This is our power to commit. It also determines the strength of our commitment. We often term the strength of this power *our willpower.*

What happens when we decide that action is warranted? Are we satisfied by having good intentions? Do we commit ourselves easily, or resist taking action even if we know it is needed? If we commit, do we follow through? Or are we easily distracted, dissuaded, or discouraged? Do we devote ourselves to carrying out our commitments and overcoming any obstacle in the process?

But solid food is for the mature, who because of practice
have their senses trained to distinguish between good and evil.
HEBREWS 5:14

GOD'S INTENTION FOR THE USE OF THESE POWERS

Can you see what God intends for us as we use these powers? He wants us to embrace the reality that His Word is true and real, His ways are right, and His plan is the most beneficial course we can choose. He wants us to recognize the importance of what is most important—first Him, then our relationship with Him and its obligations, then His will for our lives (His Lordship). He wants us to fully commit to Him, His considerations, and His plan within Covenant. Then, make every necessary effort and sacrifice to follow through with our commitments, intent on overcoming every obstacle as we walk hand in hand with God.

At the moment, though, how fully are these powers developed within us, and how well are they being used? Do we have trouble deciding what is true, or right, or best for us? Are we troubled by recurring thoughts or feelings that seem instead to control us? Do we have urges and desires that are destructive and self-sabotaging? Do we have trouble making or keeping commitments? Are we easily distracted when we do make a commitment? Are we too easily influenced by others? Is it clear that we have not strengthened these powers by proper use? In this case, God has good news! These powers can be strengthened by proper use, just like our muscles.

As you consider your life, how well-developed are these powers? How might strengthening these powers and properly using them change your life?

____

____

____

We spoke about our decision-making, and the array of voices within us that chime in when we face a decision. Where do these various ideas come from in the first place? We may hear ideas from our character, because we may have a usual way of dealing with a situation; we may hear from our guidance system for living, because this situation may relate to our goals or our strategies for success; and we may hear from our emotions, desires, values, or many other parts of the fabric of our being. Aside from God's Spirit within, **where do the other ideas within us come from the ideas we have chosen to believe? In one way or another, these come from our beliefs.**

HOW DOES AN IDEA BECOME A BELIEF?

Let's go back to our *power of assent and dissent*. **There is a doorway that leads within us that has a doorknob only on the inside.** Myriad ideas come before us every day: advice, advertising, the example of other's lives, messaging from our culture, or perhaps from God's Word. **This door is our barrier to considering an idea.**

If we have no interest in considering an idea, we keep this door firmly shut. If we are willing to consider this idea, we open the door a crack and take a look. Some ideas are quickly dismissed; some are considered, then rejected or accepted. Others undergo careful consideration before we give the thumbs-up or thumbs-down.

To decide if an idea is real, right, true, or beneficial, we match it against other things we know are true, and against our experiences and perceptions. We consider the credibility of the source of the idea. We weigh the evidence. We consider our feelings, desires, values, and other inner considerations. We consider the potential benefit this idea may have for us. After considering all pertinent factors, we render our judgment. We are all familiar with this part. But what else is also happening?

WHAT HAPPENS WITHIN US WHEN WE EMBRACE AN IDEA AS TRUTH?

Additional things happen: important, powerful, life-forming, life-changing, life-directing, but largely unnoticed things. First, when we choose to designate an idea as true, this idea comes through the doorway into our life and takes up residence. This idea becomes part of what we "know to be true" about self, life, God, and other people. This is no longer just *an idea*—it is part of *our truth.*

Ideas about a phone, food, clothing, or a car have limited impact on our inner self. But what if an idea is about how to live for best results? Or, who we are? Or, who God is? Or our fundamental relationship with other people, or our husband or wife? Or the supposed "need" to validate our self-worth with sexual activity with any willing participant? Or the consummate value of money, fame, beauty, power, or … whatever? **Do such ideas impact the course of our life? Probably more than we realize!**

When we embrace an idea, it becomes part of our frame of reference, which we use to evaluate other ideas. If we brand one idea as true and another idea conflicts with it, we often dismiss the conflicting idea as untrue without further thought.

What we decide is true impacts our relationships. How? Our feelings warm toward ideas we deem to be true, right, real, or beneficial. Or they cool toward ideas we deem to be none of the above. Our hearts then warm toward people who are wise enough to embrace the same ideas, and they cool toward the poor, deceived souls who see things differently. In fact, our beliefs are perhaps the greatest uniting or dividing factor among people.

Given the variety of ways an embraced idea impacts our inner being, how important is our decision about what we believe to be true? Why is this so?

____

____

____

We all live out our beliefs. Have you noted how different beliefs about an issue can send lives in very different directions?

____

____

____

Consider the extent to which we become what we believe. Have you noticed this reality in anyone around you … or within yourself?

____

____

____

HOW IS THE FABRIC OF OUR BEING FORMED?

Our embraced beliefs directly form our values, goals, strategies, desires, priorities, preferences (sexual and otherwise), dreams, aspirations, self-imposed limits, fears, concerns, attitudes, and judgments. **Thus, these direct our daily decision-making.**

But our embraced ideas also impact us at a deeper level. Throughout our life we decide what kind of person we should be for best results. What character qualities work best? How should we best respond to circumstances, people, and God? Thus, from the ideas we embrace about these issues we form our character. We also form our opinions about what our best life would look like and how we can get there. That is, we form our guidance system for living—from which emerges the direction of our life and our "success strategies."

We buy into **ideas about who we are**, and how we fit into the overall scheme of things. **These come together to form our self-image**. Altogether, our embraced ideas form our approach to God, other people, life, and ourselves. These ideas largely determine our experience of life. **In sum, these ideas form every element of our inner self**—with the notable exceptions of our true identity and the Spirit of God.

What parts of your inner self have been formed by what you decided to believe?

____

____

____

HOW DO WE DECIDE WHAT WE WANT?

Putting all of these pieces together, **we can now answer the important question posed earlier: "Why do we want what we want?"** We decided that certain things are real, right, true, or beneficial. We decided that certain things are important. If we decided something is both beneficial and important, we will desire this thing. The more beneficial we believe it to be, the more we will want it. As previously noted, *what we want* in turn drives a vast amount of our decision-making.

ARE WE EVER WRONG ABOUT WHAT WE BELIEVE, OR WHAT WE WANT?

I collect vintage watches. Suppose I see a beautiful, rare, and quite valuable one for sale—for a surprisingly low price. I have heard about this watch but have never seen one. Finances are tight. But when I consider this situation—I will likely never see another one for sale—I decide that this is a sacrifice worth making.

I now have the resources necessary to purchase it in my pocket. As I examine the watch, I notice how brightly the numbers on the dial glow in the dark. Upon further questioning, I learn that the numbers glow as they do because these were painted with radium. The watch is for sale because the previous owner, who enjoyed wearing the watch, recently died from leukemia. Do I buy the watch?

God gives to us the right and the responsibility to determine what is actually true. It is vital that we get these answers right, because every day we are bombarded with sales pitches for ideas and things, causes and agendas, and possible life-upgrades. **We are invited to believe, join, buy, value, give to, and devote our lives to … what?** In light of this barrage of sales pitches, how good a job do we humans do figuring out what is truly true, real, right, or beneficial? Simply consider the variety of beliefs on any topic in our world. **The firmly held beliefs of one person may conflict with, or totally contradict, the firmly held beliefs of another person. It is from this observation that we get the terms "my truth" and "your truth."**

But are these terms valid? Would be better to say instead, "What I *believe to be* true," or "What I *want to be* true"? Consider how many people load their lives down with things of little or no value, chase goals that do not satisfy in the end, do wrong things while convinced they are doing the right thing, and waste their lives in futile pursuits. Have you and I ever done such things? **Did we all embrace actual truth about these matters, or a counterfeit that masquerades as truth?**

WHERE IS OUR LIFE HEADED?

We must note an obvious reality. When we make the judgment that something is true, real, right, or beneficial, this does not ensure that it actually is any of these things. We literally bet our life and our future on our choice. But we may be wrong. I may not realize that radium is highly radioactive, or that it can cause leukemia. **I may buy, then enjoy wearing a watch that slowly destroys me, one tick at a time.**

Given the impact of embracing an idea, can you imagine the impact of embracing beliefs that are totally wrong? We literally build our inner self and the course of our lives upon these things. Fortunately, when our choices do not turn out the way we want, or relationships fall apart, or our self image leads us into dark places, or we notice character issues, all of us quickly recognize the real source of the problem, review our belief system, and correct our wrong ideas … or do we? Oddly, very few people connect wrong beliefs with unfortunate outcomes and attributes. Does this blind spot create problems for us? Instead, to what do we attribute our problems?

Experience shows that we are wrong more often than we realize. Here, another aspect of our wiring system must be emphasized: once we decide something is true and embrace it as such, **from our perspective this idea becomes more true than anything else.** In fact, this idea becomes for us *the very definition of truth*—from our perspective. **Can you see a conflict looming here when God enters the picture and offers His truth?**

Have you ever read God's Word, and felt a strong urge dismiss what He says? Why?

____

____

____

Blessed is the one who does not condemn himself by what he approves.
ROMANS 14:22

HOW WE DECIDE WHAT WE BELIEVE 2.0

If what we believe is true isn't actually true, a new idea that is in fact true will seem wrong to us. It may run cross-grain with our feelings, values, or anything else within us that was built upon a false idea. Thus, **we will feel significant internal resistance** to this new idea.

Now, suppose the new (actually true) idea we encounter comes from God. What will we want to do relative to this truth? Does this explain the resistance we feel at times when we read God's Word? We might not actually say it, but we have the sense that we have a better read on some things than God. But do we? **Where does this perception come from, and what should we do in this situation?**

"What is truth?"
PONTIUS PILATE, JUST BEFORE HE SIGNED OFF ON THE PLAN TO ASSASSINATE THE SON OF GOD
JOHN 18:38

"Then you will know the truth, and the truth will set you free."
JOHN 8:32

WHAT IS TRUTH?

We need to define what we mean by *actually true*. Something actually true is a correct description of what did happen, what is happening, or what is going to happen. **Actual truth is synonymous with reality.** Something not actually true, in contrast, is an incorrect description of something that is real, or it describes something that is not real. Other terms for such things are a lie, or a fantasy.

Our lives represent a mixture of ideas: some are actually true, some are not. Our inner selves are built upon, and directed by, this mixture. However, from our vantage point everything we have chosen to believe is (to us) the very definition of truth. And the inner self we have built upon all of this seems to us to be the best anyone could possibly do, given the circumstances.

... choosing rather to endure ill-treatment with the people of God than to enjoy the temporary pleasures of sin.
HEBREWS 11:25 (NASB)

However, as we live out the *not true* parts of our life, we run head-on into reality. Things that are in alignment with God and His ways—and reality—work well in the long run. Honesty, integrity, faithfulness, loyalty, caring—these work well in any aspect of life. God tells us that other ways—lying, stealing, using people, betraying them, misusing His gift of sexuality—never lead to a good place in the end. These may seem to benefit us in the short run. But, in the end, they never do. Why are these outcomes so predictable?

Because we live in the world God created, one that includes particular consequences for every choice we make. We get to choose our beliefs, attitudes, and actions, but we do not get to choose our consequences. God ordains those. Relationships grow, or relationships fall apart. Lives grow and flourish, or fall apart. Or they languish somewhere in the middle, mired in self-inflicted problems and regret.

Have you ever noted, or experienced, the relationship between beliefs, desires, choices, and consequences? In what way?

____

____

____

THE DIFFERENCE BETWEEN OUR PERCEPTION AND REALITY

Most of us come to God because our lives are no longer working well enough, and our inner life is in worse shape. **But we are not really sure why, because everything we have done and everything we are, in our eyes, is the best anyone could do.**

From our vantage point we cannot grasp the details of the cause-and-effect universe we inhabit **any more than Eve could see what would happen next if she ate the forbidden fruit**. Once she stood before God, and the consequences of her actions were glaringly evident, her reply was brief and to the point: "The serpent deceived me, and I ate." God refrained from saying what He might have said: "But what did I say to you?" Wouldn't it be wonderful if we could know in advance what would really work in our lives, and what would not? In fact, has God already made a considerable effort to answer this question for us? How did He do so?

This God—His way is perfect; the word of the Lord proves true;
He is a shield for all who take refuge in Him.
2 Samuel 22:31

"Sanctify them in the truth; your word is truth."
John 17:17

God offers a gift of unimaginable importance as we enter a relationship with Him. He has authored a lengthy book that explains everything that matters—that we cannot figure out on our own. We are assured by Him that everything He reveals to us in this book is absolutely true. His answers will work.

Would knowing how various decisions will turn out in the end point us toward our best life? Would this knowledge impact what you or I want? Are God's answers available to us? If so, where do we find them?

____

____

____

In our journey with God, we have the joy and privilege of looking behind the curtain at spiritual realities we could not otherwise know. These realities determine what happens in our world—and our lives. We get answers to the big questions: "Who is God?" "How did we get here?" "Who are we, and why are we here?" "What pleases God and yields blessings?" And, "What things do not please Him?" "What choices impact our current life and our eternity—and why?"

Do you believe God has revealed actual truth to us?

____

____

____

We enter the Kingdom of God in a state of confusion—about life, God, ourselves, and other people. God offers us the opportunity to cut through the confusion and see the truth.

Does it make sense to first answer this question to our satisfaction: "Is God's Word actually true?" Then, to devote ourselves to reading and studying these truths? Have you done so? If so, what difference has this made in your life? If not, what difference do you think this might make for you?

____

____

____

IS READING AND STUDYING GOD'S WORD ALL THAT IS NEEDED?

But something more is required if our lives are to change, improve, grow, and flourish. Based on our discussion to this point, what else do you think is needed? **We must embrace God's revelation of truth as *our truth*.** We must base our actions on His directions and our understanding on His revelation. We are offered this opportunity. What will we do with this chance of a lifetime?

A personal observation: Before I would give my life to Christ based on what is written in Scripture, I wrestled extensively with two questions. **"Is 'God's Word' actually from God?" And, "Is God's Word actually true, versus any other source?"** As I researched these questions, I found the available evidence to be consistent and overwhelming. The answers to both questions are clearly "Yes."

Thus, I accepted God's terms for our relationship and gave my life to Him. I also embraced the idea that His Word is superior to my own ideas if these differ, in which case I am obligated to exchange His Truth for what I thought was true. This is the ultimate proof of His Lordship over my life. Over almost five decades I have never seen His Word proven wrong, nor did I ever benefit when I departed from His Word.

Some say that trust in God's Word represents a lack of education or intelligence. In response, I note that I have post-graduate scientific training. I am a surgeon, and I have an IQ that is well above average for either physicians or scientists. In fact, I firmly believe that **God's Word offers the only sufficient explanation for everything we see within ourselves and in the world around us.** And it offers the only real hope in a world that is determined to head in wrong directions.

I say with complete confidence that we can fully trust His Word and trust in Him as our Lord. We can safely place our life and future in His loving hands.

What is your level of confidence that God's Word is the definition of truth, and that it should reasonably overrule any conflicting thought, feeling, desire, or value that resides within you or that comes from any human or supernatural source?

What questions or concerns do you still have regarding the truth of God's Word?

Please understand that **you must answer every personal question and objection** before you can be fully persuaded that God's Word is true, and fully confident that His Word is the best guide for your life. God's Word has withstood intense scrutiny before hostile examiners. His Word has proven to be reliable for thousands of years. He is not afraid of your questions. He will provide sufficient answers if you honestly seek them.

If you wanted to put together a plan to draw closer to God; to become more mature, Christlike, and loving; and to live the new life God offers—what would this plan look like? Based on our discussion to this point, outline your plan.

CHAPTER NINE

GOD'S PLAN VERSUS SATAN'S PLAN

WHERE DID THE IDEAS WE CHOOSE TO BELIEVE COME FROM?

We match any new idea against *what we already know to be true*. But where did our frame of reference come from—*our truth*, by which we evaluate the truth of everything else? Where did our values, desires, and goals—our guidance system—come from? Where did our ideas about how to act, or respond, or deal with our emotions come from? Why do we think others are just supposed to "deal with it" as we mistreat them—while we are "just being ourselves"?

In sum, where did all of the wrong things we believe, and built our lives upon, *come from in the first place?* Why were we willing to buy into things that are not true, things that turn out poorly? Can we not see how these same ideas play out all around us?

Scripture describes sharply contrasting things: God's ways (in the Kingdom of Light) versus the world's ways (the kingdom of darkness); our old life versus our new life; and the desires of the flesh versus the desires of the Spirit. Each of these contrasts refers to the same thing. **We live on a battlefield in a war between God and His enemy.**

In a war, when an enemy is devoted to our destruction, it is highly inappropriate to wear the enemy's uniform, follow his advice, advance his agenda, or encourage others to do likewise—yet this is what we do when we pursue our *old life*. During a war between nations, we term such people *traitors*, and often execute them.

God calls us to turn completely from our "old life" to our "new life." Yet, in Christian lives, do elements of these two lives often blend together? Is this as a serious problem? Please explain why, or why not.

THE WAR AROUND US AND WITHIN US

On one side is God: His ways, will, desires, truth, and plan. From our new inner life—in part created by God, in part to be built by us upon His Truth and led by His Spirit—God intends a new external life to flow that is in harmony with His life. In Covenant, we are now literally an extension of His life. God wants **the life we choose to live** to bear witness to reality—that is, **to the realities of the Covenant we entered with Him.**

On the other side is God's enemy. Satan is devoted to corrupting, then ultimately destroying those made in God's image. When we lived in his kingdom, our old nature—along with his lies, the corrupted inner being built upon his lies, and the outer life that flows from those lies—mirrored this enemy's life.

When we enter His Kingdom, God creates for us a new identity, or essence, or true self, or life. But we also carry forward into God's Kingdom the other parts of our inner self—*including the aspects which are built upon the lies of God's enemy.*

Whose life do we reflect as we continue to live out these lies?

Why is God so determined that we abandon our old life and build a new life? Because the ways of His enemy are designed to reduce, damage, and/or destroy our lives—though we are often unaware of this because we are surrounded by a world full of people who embrace the same lies, who do not realize where their lives are headed.

In this war we are both the battlefield and the prize. The weapons in this war are ideas. We get to choose from two opposing sets of ideas: God's or Satan's. The ideas we choose become our beliefs, then the fabric of our being and our way of life. **The only thing worse than being on a battlefield is being on one, but not realizing it** until—while following the enemy's guidance—we end up in a life-damaging or life-destroying situation we didn't see coming. God sees the end from the beginning. We do not.

Does Satan's influence in our lives have a predictable outcome? What, and how?

Many of Satan's directives do not look abjectly evil. His guidance may move us toward outcomes we consider—on superficial examination—to be good. Satan offers people enough actual benefits (from our limited vantage point) to gain our trust. Satan markets his ideas as "a reasonable alternative" to God's plan, and with "more upside." But his ultimate agenda is never far beneath the surface. At the very least, people suffer when they refrain from following God's plan to build their best life.

But following the voice of God's enemy always involves a progression that moves us farther and farther from God and His path. The question is not so much about the potential benefit of a particular action. Instead, the questions become: "To whom are we listening, what path are we on, and where does this path ultimately lead?" The enemy will dangle before us what we think we want, in order to take away from us what is of greatest value. In my family, we refer to these things as "fishing lures."

What impact does it have on us if we do "good things" that are not God's things?

____

____

____

God says to choose carefully to whom we listen and who we follow. But we do not see the big picture that God sees. We are not so sure. We've done pretty well so far, haven't we? We may think, "My life needs a few minor adjustments, and a bit of God's power and love, and I'll be just fine." Until we're not … because we did not listen to God and faithfully do what He says. **God tells us to take off our old life and put on our new one for one extremely good reason: because He loves us.**

Do you at times prefer your old life and resist God's call to change? If so, why?

____

____

____

Do you sometimes turn from your old life and live out your new one? When you do so, why are you willing to make these changes? What outcomes have you noted?

____

____

____

____

____

____

How can we know whether something belongs to our old life, or our new one?

____

____

____

You were taught, with regard to your former way of life, to put off your old self which is being corrupted by its deceitful desires; to be made new in the attitude of your minds; and to put on the new self, created to be like God in true righteousness and holiness.

EPHESIANS 4:22-24

HOW DO WE REMOVE ONE LIFE AND PUT ANOTHER IN ITS PLACE?

To take down a large structure—like the life we have built to this point—it helps to understand **what is holding up the building**. We may bring in a sledgehammer or bulldozer and start chipping away … with limited impact. Or we can attack the key elements that hold up the building. If we know what these key elements are made of, and we apply a force that removes their strength, the building will fall. To succeed in the task before us, we must understand what is needed to successfully remove the support structure of our old life. Then we can use a similar strategy to build our new life upon a firm foundation. To do this, God offers the following instruction:

Therefore I urge you, brothers and sisters, by the mercies of God, to present your bodies as a living and holy sacrifice, acceptable to God, which is your spiritual service of worship. And do not be conformed to this world, but be transformed by the renewing of your mind, so that you may prove what the will of God is, that which is good and acceptable and perfect.

ROMANS 12:1, 2 (NASB)

… since you stripped off the old self with its evil practices and have put on the new self, which is being renewed to a true knowledge according to the one who created it.

COLOSSIANS 3:9, 10

In these verses, God uses the phrases "transformed by the renewing of your mind" and "renewed to a true knowledge." These refer to a process that is not further described. In order to understand what God is instructing us to do, we must see the relationship between an idea—and the choice to believe this idea—and the formation of our mind, heart, and will. And the formation of our character, guidance system, and self-image. Together, these determine the life we live. Whose ideas we choose—God's or Satan's—in turn determines whether we remain affixed to our old life, or build our new one. Please describe in your own words the process of transformation God mentions in the above verses.

THE WEAPONS IN THIS SPIRITUAL WAR: TRUTH VERSUS LIES

An idea is in reality either true, right, real, or beneficial … or it is not. Scripture describes God as the source of all truth. Satan, in contrast, is termed "the father of lies." We can simply call the not-true ideas we previously embraced "lies." **Humanity had never heard a lie until Satan showed up**. What role does he still play today in the lies we have embraced and still live out?

THE ENEMY'S PLAYBOOK

If you were Satan and wanted to do as much damage to your life as possible, what strategy would you use? Has Satan devoted himself to loading all of humanity down with a vast number of false ideas about God, life, ourselves, and other people? He watches with delight when we resist God as He tries to lead us to our best life, then inundates us with even more reasons to resist God.

THE IMPORTANT THINGS WE DON'T NOTICE

Though our lives are a mixture of good and bad ideas, and all that is built upon them, we often go nose-blind to the bad. We comfort ourselves by noting now much worse things—or we—could be. We must understand: this is the life God instructs us to move away from. Why? Because **God has a very different life waiting for us.**

For the flesh desires what is contrary to the Spirit, and the Spirit what is contrary to the flesh. They are in conflict with each other, so you are not to do whatever you want.
GALATIANS 5:17

The one who sows to please his flesh, from the flesh will reap destruction.
GALATIANS 6:8

SATAN'S SECRET WEAPON: OUR OWN WIRING SYSTEM

Even if we say "Jesus is Lord," and want to follow Him, something within us pushes back. **It turns out Satan has a secret weapon. He uses the way God created our inner wiring system to form a reservoir of resistance to God within us.** How? Consider how Scripture describes "our flesh": as the source of evil desires.

Changing from our old life to our new life is not just a true-false test. The real question comes down to *our desires.* What do we really want? **Satan has learned how to get us to *want what he tells us to want*—**which is always to **turn away from God's leadership**.

Let's take a closer look at how Satan does this.

TRUTH VERSUS DECEPTION

What is deception? In short, a deception is a lie that *we believe to be true.* But a deception is more than a lie. It is a lie with a promise attached—and a price tag. Being deceived involves a process. We have a picture of this process—the emotional manipulation, the lie, and the promise—in Genesis 3:1-19.

Eve had never previously questioned the love or character of her God. He created her and her husband in a literal paradise, in which they were intended to live eternally. Then Satan took her on a journey that led her to make a choice—based on the promise of a better life. **But, instead of the promised better life, Satan's recommended path led only to death**—ultimately to physical death, but immediately to separation from God and the blessings He had lovingly provided. Note this pattern!

First, Satan attacked and discredited God's love. He implied that God is the type of being who would hold back the best from her, instead of faithfully giving her what is best for her. Eve did leap to God's defense … sort of. But she was clearly impacted by Satan's "revelation" about God's character—because she misquoted God. With Eve off-balance, Satan now bluntly stated that God is a liar. His prohibition (to not eat the fruit of the tree of the knowledge of good and evil) simply kept her from living her best life—which, according to the deceiver, was to become "like God."

Offered this opportunity for a "life upgrade," Eve was faced with a choice. The choice on one hand was about who was more credible—God, or this new being who never bothered to introduce himself. On the other hand, her choice was about *what she wanted most.* This offer clearly kindled an intense desire. Would she settle for her current life, or reach out and **take hold of a future that could be so much more?**

So Eve decided to scrutinize this situation—sort of. God had revealed a spiritual reality to her that she now discounted (because she had already put God's words in the "not beneficial" basket). So **what information was left to examine?** The question in Eve's mind was reduced to: "Based on what I can determine with my five senses in this moment, does this fruit look dangerous, or not?" She concluded from her extremely limited vantage point that the fruit appeared to be safe. In reality, though, **hadn't she already made her decision before she walked toward the tree?**

When she reached the tree, her misquote of God's prohibition **allowed her to further discredit God.** She told Satan that she "could not eat the fruit or touch the tree, lest she die." But God never said she could not touch the tree! She could put up a swing or build a treehouse in that tree if she wanted. She was only told not to eat its fruit.

But as Eve leaned against the tree, grabbed a piece of fruit with her hand, squeezed it, smelled it, perhaps snapped it off for a closer look—and did not die on the spot—her "confusion" aligned with Satan's accusation and offered credibility to his viewpoint. This experience—encountering no ill effect from her supposed violation of God's word—likely overcame any remaining reluctance she may have felt about violating God's instructions. Regardless, any consequences **were now a risk worth taking** in light of **the possible reward she had in her mind,** courtesy of God's enemy (and her enemy).

Eve chose which "truth" to embrace as *her truth.* Based upon her *new truth*—and her *new desire*—she chose to act. Humanity has paid an inestimable price for this choice ever since.

I say this so that no one will deceive you with persuasive arguments.
COLOSSIANS 2:4 (NASB)

Satan's approach was to present Eve with a series of implied questions. Then he guided her toward his desired conclusions. "Does God really love you?" Apparently not. "Does His plan for you produce your best life?" No. "Is God telling you the truth when He restricts your behaviors?" No, God is not telling the truth. "Is there another source you can consult, one who will lead you to your truly best life?" At this point, Eve's answer was, "Yes, and apparently that choice is you, Satan. Thank you for clearing up my confusion about what is truly best for me. Oh, and . . . should I peel it first, or just eat it with the skin on?"

What benefits are you pursuing in your life that you know God will not provide for you according to His plan? Or do you seek something "good" in ways that God does not endorse? If so, where do you think such a "plan" actually comes from?

____

____

____

SATAN'S ENDURING AND SUCCESSFUL STRATEGY

Is the same pattern evident today in our culture—and in our own mind and heart? **This scenario illustrates the vital role God's revelation should play in our lives.** God gave Eve information about the consequences of eating "the fruit of the tree of the knowledge of good and evil" that was not available to her through her own senses. Absent this information, or discounting it, as Eve did, are we now an easy target for God's enemy? In light of this, how would you describe our culture—**which has completely discounted virtually every aspect of God's revelation?**

...but each person is tempted when they are dragged away by their own evil desire and enticed. Then, after desire has conceived, it gives birth to sin; and sin, when it is full-grown, gives birth to death.
JAMES 1:14, 15

Consider all the things God says are evil or wrong in Scripture. Then consider how those "out of bounds" attitudes and behaviors are handled in our culture—by people who do not see what is coming next any more than Eve did.

Does understanding the spiritual war help us understand the tug of war within us—between God's Word and our competing desires? How powerful a force can our desire be if it opposes God's will for our life? Have you experienced this?

Have you noted the connection between a sales pitch to engage in ungodly behaviors and a desire kindled within us that is based on the supposed benefit of ungodly choices? In Scripture this is termed "temptation." How does our discussion help us understand the process of temptation/deception?

Is it clear that the *material* that supports our "old life" is *our choice to believe* ideas that *are not true,* and *are not from God*? This, plus the *desires* and the *inner being* based upon these lies? And, that the correct strategy to remove the strength that binds us to our *"old life"* is to *identify, reject, and eject* Satan's lies, then to *embrace as our new truth* the truths of God? What are your thoughts on this strategy? Will this approach work?

Why is God so determined that we identify and reject the leadership of His enemy? Does this explain why attempting to pay some attention to God's Lordship, while maintaining parts of our old life, is a very dangerous strategy? Can the question "Who is our Lord?" have two answers?

____

____

____

Who is your true Lord (or lord)? How is this evident in your life?

____

____

Is this the life you want, under the Lordship you really want? Yes _____. No _____.

If your answer is "No," what is your next move?

____

____

____

If with Christ you have died to the elemental spirits of the world, why ...
Colossians 2:20

... but the things that the nations sacrifice—they sacrifice to demons and not to God; and I do not wish you to come into the fellowship of the demons.
I Corinthians 10:20 (Literal Standard Version)

THE WELLSPRING FROM WHICH FLOWS ALL HUMAN MISERY

Every bit of human misery, ever since the Garden of Eden, has flowed directly from a combination of three things. First, from **humanity's loss of oneness with God**. Second, from **receiving the nature of God's enemy**—for doing so pushes individuals toward rebellious and destructive acts. Third, **from additional deceptive instructions about living that have been offered by Satan** and one-third of the angels, who followed Satan in his rebellion.

The Lord saw how great the wickedness of the human race had become, and that every inclination of the thoughts of the human heart was only evil all the time. The Lord regretted that He had made human beings on the earth and was deeply troubled.
Genesis 6:5, 6

GOD SHARPLY CONTRASTS HIS KINGDOM WITH "THE WORLD"

These fallen angels became the pantheon of gods of every culture in the ancient world. Humanity worshipped and served these "gods" because people believed (with some justification) that these beings held people's destinies in their hands. Humanity obeyed these gods, served them, and sacrificed to them. In this way, life in the ancient world was extensively formed and fashioned by fallen angels. Leaders ruled and waged war, and people loved, lived, and died in the name of their gods.

What life did this produce in individuals and cultures? The Roman Empire was built for the benefit of a small minority of "citizens" on the backs of the vast majority—who were slaves. The monumental buildings built by this labor force were purchased by ruinous taxation of their subject territories—which represented 20 percent of the ancient world. Women and children were regarded as property. Unwanted children were left to die on barren hillsides. The Romans, though, were the most civilized of the lot. **They viewed the rest of the much-less-civilized world as "barbarians."**

The Old Testament details the way of life produced by serving these gods, and strongly contrasts it with the life God intended for Israel. Against God's strongest command, these same practices crept into God's chosen people as they turned to worship these gods. Scripture describes "clearing the Temple" of resident male and female prostitutes (2 Kings 23:7). Archeologists have found remains of burned infant skeletons just outside Jerusalem's wall—tiny ones who were sacrificed to these gods. Scripture describes other behaviors that flowed from this forbidden worship, all of which were diametrically opposed to God's Law—which is no surprise given the true identity of these "gods" (noted above, 1 Corinthians 10:20 and Colossians 2:20).

The term "the world" is often used in Scripture; it is never a compliment. "The ways of the world" are listed in many places in Scripture (Ephesians 2:2; Romans 12:2; 2 Peter 1:4; Matthew 18:7). These behaviors are identical to the ways of life under the influence of fallen angels, which contrast sharply with the way of life in God's Kingdom.

How does God view "the world" we inhabit—that to a degree also inhabits us? Do you view the world, and the parts of yourself that are fashioned according to the ways of the world, in the same way God does? Why or why not?

____

____

____

We know that we are children of God, and the whole world is under the control of the evil one.
1 John 5:19

Today we optimistically await a better world, one that will be "delivered to our doorstep" by the latest advances in science, technology, and education. Are we there yet? Are we getting closer? Do humans consistently devote themselves to the benefit of others, or do most people view others with callous indifference as they pursue their own "best interests"? Do people often damage, dominate, and manipulate others? Is every blessing and resource that God created for us—from environmental resources to sexuality—often turned to purposes that degrade, damage, and destroy?

Do these "human nature" issues actually reflect the influence of God's enemy? Does Satan in fact still have a stranglehold on our current world? The gods/fallen angels who influenced the ancient world are immortal. These beings are still present in our realm whether we see them or not. **Are their fingerprints still all over every current culture's beliefs and agendas?**

What term do we use to describe our civilization? **Western civilization.** What is the foundation of this way of life? A significant Judeo-Christian influence is still present in our culture, though it is under continuing assault. But our other cultural beliefs and traditions came from a different source: from ancient Greece, through Rome, then through western Europe into the Americas. Where did the ancient Greeks and Romans derive their way of life? Or the Norse, Germanic tribes, and other original European civilizations? **Their way of life was a gift from their gods—a gift, sadly, that keeps on giving.**

Where did our current cultural values come from: "get rich," "be famous," "win at all costs," "dominate," "get my way," and all the others? Why do we want what we want? What does our culture view as true, real, right, and beneficial? What things are of greatest value? How many of our cultural priorities and beliefs align with God and His ways? From where did the rest arise? **How much of the remainder aligns instead with the character, ways, and agenda of Satan?**

Scripture sharply contrasted "the world" thousands of years ago with the Kingdom of Israel, then with the Kingdom of God that came through Jesus the Messiah. Is it of any more benefit for us to follow Satan's ways now than it was two thousand years ago? **Or is a lie still a lie--even if these are lies we firmly believe to be true?**

Each day we contend—not only with our limited point-of-view and over-estimation of our ability to chart the best course for our lives—but also with an enemy who is fiercely determined to dissuade and persuade us. He builds and cultivates desires within us through false "reasons." He has used this strategy throughout human history to create untold misery in human lives and our world. What is your personal experience with deception—ideas you thought were true, bought into, and acted on … that later did serious damage to you or others?

____

____

____

When we see these unfortunate outcomes, what do we always say? "If only I had listened to … " But, listened to what? What source of information would have kept us and others safe from this misdirection? How can this insight help us?

WHAT IS SATAN'S ULTIMATE POINT?

To counter Satan's efforts, we must be able to "dust for fingerprints." If we understand the ultimate point he is trying to make, and the ways he approaches humanity, **we are better armed to recognize and resist His efforts.**

By rebelling against the rule of God, Satan is attempting to establish his own rule over God's creation. This translates into: "Whatever God says, do the opposite." Satan's ultimate point is to create an alternate universe—at least in our minds and hearts—that aligns with **the fantasy life that led him to rebel against his Creator.**

In Satan's imaginary universe: the truths of God are no longer true; the things God says are real are not real; God is the bad guy and Satan is the good guy; Satan, as the head and ruler, now makes the rules. Good becomes the new evil, and things God says are evil are now good. God's ordained consequences **will not occur (including those directed toward Satan). Instead, we should all follow Satan to a grand and glorious new life**—as we march alongside him over the edge of the cliff.

SATAN WANTS NO CREDIT FOR HIS INFLUENCE IN OUR LIVES

For Satan's plan to succeed in the life of Christians, we must continue to want him and his rule—without actually realizing what we are doing. How does this occur? We simply continue to live "my life" as a Christian. We follow our old desires, pursue our old agendas, and live our old dreams without further thought.

Satan is not interested in intellectual property rights. He is delighted when people broadcast and implement all of his ideas without acknowledging their source. He is especially delighted, no doubt, when his ideas are taught in seminary classrooms, then broadcasted from pulpits across our land.

How can we "dust for fingerprints" to distinguish between God's intentions and Satan's ideas so we can avoid promoting Satan's agenda?

Many will object to the view that Satan's leadership and ideas have this kind of impact on our world and our lives. None of us actually see Satan whispering lies into the ears of the unsuspecting. But if we understand the principles and practices of the ancient world and how they worshiped their gods, and match these principles and practices against our current cultural trends—the correlation is striking.

Consider, for instance, the "sexual revolution" that occurred during my seventy-year lifetime. Turning sexuality from a "within Covenant" activity into a supposed "recreational, casual" activity has predictably produced what consequences? For one, the creation of a large number of children via this misuse of sexuality. This, in turn, led to a remarkably passionate drive to sacrifice these young lives, to supposedly "improve the lives" of prospective mothers. Human sacrifice in the name of "the gods" was a widespread feature of the ancient world, as was turning sexuality away from God's intent toward the various mis-uses we see throughout history, and in our culture.

We can solve a crime by dusting for fingerprints or checking for DNA left behind. It is not necessary to see a perpetrator actually commit the crime. Whose DNA and fingerprints are found all over "the world"—throughout history, and today?

When Adam and Eve redirected their worship to Satan, they didn't build a temple or offer a sacrifice to him. **They simply listened to his directions and followed them.** Neither do we need to enter a pagan temple to worship God's enemy. We simply turn on a screen. The same teachings are delivered straight to us—and our children. Does anyone in our culture follow this voice? There is truly nothing new under the sun.

"Then you will know the truth, and the truth will set you free."
JOHN 8:32

Love must be sincere. Hate what is evil, cling to what is good.
ROMANS 12:9

The reason the Son of God appeared was to destroy the devil's work.
1 JOHN 3:8

Similar to the way that desires are formed and fueled by our belief about benefit, we form other emotions in response to our understanding of risk, danger, and damage. Once we cut through the confusion, and truly understand the risk, danger, and damage that flow from Satan's guidance, how should we reasonably feel when we see this influence in our world, our Christian community, or our own life? What desires should our understanding form, and energize? What passions should this arouse? What decisions and commitments are reasonable, and what actions should we take?

Jesus came to deliver us from all of this. How can we assist Him in this task?

____

____

____

CHAPTER TEN

THE FLESH VERSUS LOVING AS GOD LOVES

For the flesh desires what is contrary to the Spirit, and the Spirit what is contrary to the flesh. They are in conflict with each other, so that you are not to do whatever you want.
GALATIANS 5:17

Satan incessantly attacks God and the things of God. In terms of our individual lives, though, Scripture directs our attention toward his key attack-point within us: the flesh. When this term is used in reference to Christians, the flesh is depicted as **the primary force within us that opposes God's will.**

Our flesh is thus the primary obstacle hindering the development of the new life God desires. When the term "the flesh" is used in this way, **it refers to all the elements of one's inner life that are built upon and directed by the lies of God's enemy.**

For those who slip through Satan's fingers and exit his kingdom, Satan has a powerful fallback strategy: **to inactivate us as Christians through confusion and internal conflict**—from which will flow inconsistent behavior and interpersonal conflict. As a result, many end up with a small fraction of the life God actually offers within Covenant.

Our flesh is a combination of two things: First, ideas that originated from Satan. Second, our agreement with these ideas. To counter Satan's strategy, we must understand what he has already done to us, and what we in turn have done to ourselves … by simply agreeing with Satan about what to believe and how to live.

If we are asked, "How many ideas that we base our life upon came from Satan?"—could we come up with any? But if the question is asked another way—"How many ideas that you base your life

upon are out of sync with God's Word or will?" —perhaps we can indeed come up with at least a few. Can you think of any?

____

____

____

Instead of questioning God's Word, the most important and constructive thing we can do at that point is to question our belief system. Specifically, we need to recognize the original source of beliefs that are out-of-sync with God. If we do, we are much more likely to exchange the deceptive guidance of our enemy for the truth of God. But what if we remain clueless as to the source of our resistance?

Satan is much smarter than we are. **He has learned to cloak his control of our lives beneath the fabric of our own being.** How often will we do what God says to do if our inner being strongly resists doing so? If someone asks us a question about following God, we will say, "I want to follow God!" We may believe we have the best of intentions if we inquire within ourselves. But deep within, if we really want something other than what God wants, how does this play out in practice? Are we unremittingly faithful to God, as Covenant requires? Or are we something else?

Have you ever experienced this kind of inner tug-of-war—between what God wants and what you want? How did this play out in your life?

____

____

____

Let's take a closer look at the inner force that periodically redirects control of our lives from God and His Lordship back into the hands of Satan.

But each person is tempted when they are dragged away by their own evil desire and enticed.
James 1:14

Now these things happened as examples for us so that we would
not crave evil things as they indeed craved them.
I Corinthians 10:6

FROM SATAN'S LIPS MAY COME OUR STRONGEST DESIRES

We desire what we believe is beneficial for us. If we perceive something to be of great value, the strength of our desire is in proportion to its perceived value. If we believe something is a vital part of our best life, how do we feel about it? To what lengths will we go to get something we deeply desire?

Why has Satan spent millennia selling humanity on the supposed benefits of various ungodly activities? Does it make sense that Satan's first move with Eve was to portray living eternally in God's paradise as only her second-best choice?

When we strongly desire something, beneath this urge is always the belief that what we desire will provide tremendous benefit. **At the same time, we dismiss and discard approaches that we believe are of little benefit. Satan has worked tirelessly to persuade us that faithfulness to God falls into the latter category.**

FROM SATAN'S LIPS MAY COME OUR STRONGEST RELUCTANCE

We must recognize within ourselves, then, **not only desires that have been formed to have things in our life that God does not want us to have, but also an aversion to the life God wants us to lead.** Recall the impact of Satan's words on Eve. She inhabited a literal paradise in a perfect marriage with an ideal husband. She walked with her God, physically and in every other way, in a relationship of "oneness." She would continue all of this for eternity, unless … How could someone in the most favorable possible situation throw it all away, to reach for … ?

In the same way, **why would we possibly refrain from building the new life God offers**, learning to obey Him in all things, learning to love as He loves, learning to walk with Him in the way Eve and Adam desperately wished they could still do …

Are we going to let our flesh call the shots in our life, and continue to hold us away from the life God intends for us in all of its fullness? Or are we going to find the way to the life God re-created us to live, by properly identifying, understanding, and overcoming our flesh—this evil, rebellious influence within ourselves?

What kinds of things do we deeply desire, and what kinds of things do we shy away from, based on Satan's marketing campaign?

____

____

____

WHAT GOD'S STRATEGY TO OVERCOME THE FLESH IS NOT

Is the path to success simply to resist urges that push us in ungodly directions? Is the answer to "just say no!" to sin? While we should use our willpower to obey, we must understand **why this approach alone is insufficient in many situations.**

Have you ever tried very hard to resist a sinful choice, but failed to consistently do so? Does our discussion help us understand why we failed? In what way?

____

____

____

We are contending with our own belief system. We are already convinced that certain things are true, right, real, or beneficial. Our own voice commends these beliefs. Each deceptive idea is accompanied by another belief—**in the long-term benefit of carrying out this idea. This supposed benefit is what we really want.** For each deceptive idea, our heart has its eyes on the prize—even if early results are disappointing. We have already committed ourselves to pay the price for this prize—one we now covet. In Scripture God describes such ungodly pursuits as *idols*. What an interesting term!

Suppose we are deceived at some point—convinced that Satan's words are true. What now? We must look up and see the big picture. **The idea itself, and the belief in its benefit, are lies straight from the pit of hell.** Would we fly to Colombia and ask the head of a cartel for advice about life? Why, then, would we look to an even more malicious and destructive source—the head of the rebellion against God—and base our life upon his hate-filled advice that is designed to lure us to destruction?

This makes no sense, but we all do it. *Another name for Satan's advice, lived out, is our "old life."* This is the life that we preferred, that we chose—because in our mind and heart we were firmly convinced that this is the best life available to us. That is, until God opens our eyes to two key realities: 1) what Satan has done to us; and 2) what we did to ourselves by embracing his guidance.

Any desire built upon Satan's ideas is by definition an evil desire. We may look within ourselves and disagree that "evil things" are within us, because we have no desire to torture or murder someone, or to commit a grossly immoral act. *But here we must consider the true definition of evil.*

Any desire that prompts us to rebel against the Lordship of Christ is by definition evil. Why? Because each such idea is designed to damage us and/or others. We may vigorously argue for the benefit of these things—just as Eve would have passionately explained why she should eat the forbidden fruit after Satan "informed" her it was good to do so. **But she was wrong in her assessment—and so are we when we are "informed" by this same source.**

Have you ever been convinced that something would be so beneficial and important—even necessary for your best life—and yet none of this proved to be true in the end?

____

____

____

How do we overcome evil desires? If we want something badly enough to disobey God, or find ourselves saying, "I know I shouldn't, but … "; or, "I know I should, but … " If a desire is strong enough to overrule our "better judgment," is this is a call to action?

What action would you recommend to a friend who is facing this situation?

If we simply resist things within us that push back against God, our "success" will only be partial—and mostly represent legalistic rule-keeping. **We will not accomplish the internal renovation and transformation upon which our new life must be built**—instead, the flesh within us will remain, and continue to be a source of opposition.

Is the path away from evil desires also the path toward the inner transformation God wants for us? Is this truly the path toward our best life? What do you think?

GOD'S ACTUAL STRATEGY

A deception only has power as long as we continue to embrace it as true. Rebellious urges and the evil desires of our flesh remain active and powerful until we review—and reject—the ideas upon which these desires were based in the first place. We are all capable of spotting the lie in a deceptive sales pitch—if we bother to look. **If we know an idea is a lie, will we follow it? No, we will not.**

Does this offer us a powerful tool that can dismantle the resistance to God—one evil desire after another? This is the tool God instructs us to use in His Covenant plan. This is what it means to be "transformed by the renewing of our mind."

What will happen if we **re-examine each idea upon which ungodly desires are based, spot the lies in Satan's sales pitches, then reject these lies and divorce ourselves from them?**

Then, what if we find God's truth on the matter, embrace His Word as our truth, and acknowledge the huge importance and benefit of doing things God's way? **If we do this, will we replace each evil desire with a desire for the things of God?**

Based on what we have learned, do you believe this strategy will work? Why or why not?

If we engage in this process on an ongoing basis, one issue after another, will we rebuild our character—one mis-formed character quality at a time? Will we reconstruct and redirect our guidance system? Will we develop a whole new set of strategies for living? Will our self-image come into alignment with reality? Will our emotions begin to function properly and come into alignment with God's heart? **This is why God instructs us to rebuild every aspect of our life that we misconstructed in the first place, so that our whole life progressively comes into alignment with His life.**

Is the relationship now clear between our beliefs, our choices, our desires, our character qualities, our life direction, our strategy for living, our self-image, our preferences and urges, our values, our frame of reference, and "our truth"? Are you beginning to see these connections within yourself? If so, in what ways?

You were taught ... to put off your old self ... and to put on the new self ...
EPHESIANS 4:22,24

OUT WITH THE OLD, IN WITH THE NEW!

Are the next necessary steps now apparent? If we can remove things within ourselves that resist God, we can also **insert beliefs, and all that is built upon these beliefs, within ourselves—beliefs that will be in harmony with God's Word, character, and plan for our lives. This process rebuilds our "inner self" and redirects our way of life according to the plan and purposes of God.**

Do not be conformed to this world, but be transformed by the renewing of your mind, that you may prove what the will of God is, that which is good, and acceptable, and perfect.
ROMANS 12:2

This life-long process is literally the most rewarding thing we will ever do, but it is also among the most difficult tasks we will ever undertake. To be willing to make the massive, sustained effort this process requires, **we must understand the massive benefit of this process.** This is literally the only way that the life-changes God calls for can occur. We must remove our internal resistance to the changes called for by God, **or any changes will be, at best, partial—and opposition will remain.**

To love as God directs, to emulate the life of Christ, to faithfully live out our Covenant with God, we must **replace our resistance to God with a desire, an urge, a hunger for God and the things of God.** Everything within us must want to see our life accurately reflect the life of Christ. Or we will not do so—because we will not want to do so. **Is this process of inner transformation the true path—the only path—to our best life?**

What would be required to shift from an evil desire to a godly desire for a particular issue in your life?

____

____

____

It is possible for us to build within ourselves an ever-stronger desire for God and the things of God. What would be required to do this?

____

____

____

Would the time and effort required to do the above be well spent? Why?

____

____

____

But godliness with contentment is great gain.
I Timothy 6:6

A "TRANSFORMED MIND" IMPACTS OUR EXPERIENCE OF LIFE

Through this process of inner transformation we are describing, we make great strides toward internal coherence. Why? Because our beliefs come into alignment with each other, and with God. What we believe is *actually true.* What we believe is real, is *actually real.* What we believe to be beneficial produces good results, and allows God to bless us. The parts of our inner self now function as a *coordinated whole*—in harmony with God's Spirit and the realities of life.

If our character, guidance system, and self-image align with truth, God, and each other, what life will we most deeply desire?

The flesh desires what is contrary to the Spirit, and the Spirit what is contrary to the flesh. They are in conflict with each other, so that you may not do whatever you want.
GALATIANS 5:17

IF THIS IS NOT OUR EXPERIENCE OF LIFE, CONSIDER WHY THIS IS SO

Lies that we embrace pull us in a direction. Each belief pulls us toward one thing or another. In sum, a confused array of beliefs pulls us in many directions at once. All of them pull us away from God, and away from what God wants to do in and through us. If we want to move "toward God," do we find ourselves tethered in place? Do many people feel "stuck" in places they do not want to be? Could this be why?

If we have wrong goals and agendas, encounter negative consequences of wrong choices, and misunderstand the nature of our best life, what kind of life do we have? Instead of the life of God, we have anxiety, discontent, insecurity, frustration, anger, and bitterness. We dislike others and are disliked. We hate and are hated. We damage others and ourselves. God's Spirit within and our own conscience continue to bear witness of our shame and guilt. At the same time, through it all we perceive ourselves as a victim. **How many wrong beliefs are evident in all of this?**

Can we cleanse ourselves from these things? If so, how can this be done?

IF IT ISN'T BROKE, DON'T FIX IT ...

Clearly, not everything within us is wrong. The transformation God calls for does not include things within us that are already in alignment with Him—character qualities, values, life direction, and more. Things that are already built upon His truths will serve us well, and God.

So put to death and deprive of power the evil longings of your earthly body ...
Colossians 3:5 (Amplified Bible)

IF IT IS BROKE, PLEASE DO ...

We must deal with a life-long perception problem, one that exists because of how God created our inner workings. Things within us that are actually wrong may still seem right to us. If we cannot trust our perception to tell us when we are right or wrong, how will we know when something needs to be adjusted? **We know this if we face an internal struggle to obey God.** At this point our resistance—our flesh—must be called out and examined.

A BIGGER PICTURE OF OUR DESIRE, BEYOND INDIVIDUAL ISSUES ...

There is another way Satan continues to hold us in his grasp that we must understand if we are to successfully divorce ourselves from desiring his life.

How do we feel about *totally divorcing ourselves* from the world and our old life? Or about being totally, and only, committed to God and His plan for our lives? Do we feel a tinge of reluctance? Why do we feel this way?

____

____

____

In the depths of our being, all of us, **if we are honest, have significant affection toward many things in our world.** This can be a bit confusing, because the world we inhabit has many good things that God created for us to enjoy. We should love and appreciate these things.

In the same way that the term *the flesh* can be confusing—meaning different things in different contexts—so the term "the world" in Scripture often does not mean the entirety of our earthly home. **It refers to the kingdom of darkness that was inserted within God's creation.** This term refers to the nature, mind, heart, will, and ways of those within Satan's kingdom. This term refers to every person who is not in a Covenant relationship with Christ, and to the rebellious spiritual forces aligned with Satan.

The mind governed by the flesh is death ... The mind governed by the flesh is hostile to God; it does not submit to God's law, nor can it do so. Those who are in the realm of the flesh cannot please God.
Romans 8:6-8

In this passage God makes ***the mind governed by the flesh*** **synonymous with Satan's power and influence.** Therefore, this term is also synonymous with *the world* and *the kingdom of darkness.* God calls us to identify the members and ways of Satan's kingdom, and to **make a clean break—to display no allegiance whatsoever to this rebellious and unwanted force within God's creation.**

Is there a greater insult to God, who did so much to deliver us from the grip of His enemy, than to continue bowing down to this same evil and rebellious influence? Yet, despite what God says, we are often confused about which life is most beneficial for us. We retain some degree of yearning for the things of the world.

How can we separate in our mind and heart the beneficial aspects of God's creation that He wants us to use and enjoy, versus Satan's realm and influence?

____

____

____

There is one more reason why we maintain affection for the world, a reason we must understand if we are to finally release our grip on our old life. For we must do this if we are to fully commit ourselves to follow God, build our new life, and learn to love as God loves within His Kingdom!

SATAN'S ULTIMATE SECRET WEAPON— AND HOW TO COUNTER IT

We have seen how Satan co-opts our God-given mechanisms of choice, belief, and inner development and uses them to his advantage. **But he has found a way to co-opt an even more powerful mechanism: our capacity to love, and to remain faithful within a Covenant relationship.** How does Satan use these capacities to keep us in his grasp?

LET'S FIRST REVIEW A FEW THINGS ABOUT LOVE

- Love is our deepest need and the wellspring of our strongest desire.
- Love is ultimately the most powerful force within us.
- Love can prompt our strongest commitments and most powerful actions.
- Love can be directed; it is a choice we must make.
- We choose to love, or refrain from loving, for reasons that we deem sufficient.

- Love takes what we believe and forms whom (or what) we believe in. This in turn determines to whom, or what, we will devote our lives.
- Love bonds us and joins us to people, ideas, or things.
- Love brings the parts of us into alignment and directs them toward a single purpose.
- Through our choices—to believe, believe in, commit our lives, then devote our lives—we define ourselves and direct our lives.
- The commitment of love translates into willingness to give, sacrifice, endure, and overcome any objection, adversity, or reversal for the sake of our beloved.

WE ARE CREATED TO LOVE

God created all of us with a profound need to give and receive love. Love is more than desire. Love is more than esteeming someone or something. When we love, we attach and join ourselves to the object of our love. Our lives are *all about* the object of our love. Our love becomes our center, the integrating point of life around which all else revolves. **Our sense of identity wraps itself around** the object of our love. We are willing to refashion ourselves for the sake of love—to do, to learn, to become **whatever is needed for the sake of our beloved.**

All of this is to say that God created us for Covenant, and Covenant was created for us. Note how our God-given capacities mirror God's intent within Covenant. Our capacity to love is, in essence, our capacity to be faithful within Covenant and build a love-for-a-lifetime relationship. **A heart full of love wants to do all that God tells us to do within Covenant.** What could possibly go wrong here?

Love is intended to be mutual. Two are fully committed to each other. But this is one of the uncertainties of love. **One who appears to offer to us his or her love** may in fact be doing so. Or they may be misleading us—and have an entirely different purpose in mind. How do we know?

Often, for a considerable period of time, we do not know. One may choose to be "all in," while the other lags back—but eventually joins in with mutual commitment. Or, we may be led on with loving words, but the heart and the actions never follow. Regarding love, what we see, feel, think, want, hope, and assume about the object of our love may be correct. Or, we may be mistaken. Or, we may be deceived. It takes time to learn the truth. **We discover the answer only through experience.**

Thus, **we are wired to persevere in our love even in the face of an uncertain outcome.** We continue to try to win the other's heart and affection even if our love is not returned—at least for a while. This is a vital element of our wiring, for two may choose to love at different times. But this is also a vulnerability, for **we may not recognize that our love will never be returned.**

True love will be proven in the trials of life—as we are loved in the ways called for by Covenant. Or, as life plays out, we may see a mismatch between the promise and the performance. We may be let down or betrayed. We may see that the other is not who we thought they are. We misread or were misled. We do well to keep all of this in mind in light of any affection we feel toward the things of the world.

Do you have personal experience with the staying power of love in the face of uncertainty? How did this turn out in the end?

HOW DO WE KNOW WHAT OR WHOM WE LOVE?

What, or whom, are we all about? What do we call ourselves? What are we devoted to? What are we willing to pay any price for? What is our top priority? What are we passionate about? What are we willing to change for the sake of ...

Take a moment to list the things you love.

The inner mechanisms we described work well if we see God as the Author of our best life, commit ourselves to Him, embrace His truth as our plan, devote ourselves to His plan, then—together with Him—build the life He intends for us.

HOW DOES SATAN USE OUR CAPACITY TO LOVE AGAINST US?

How can Satan co-opt, divert, sabotage, and misdirect our God-created wiring system and capacities? More easily than we might hope and more powerfully than we probably realize, to do far more damage to us and our lives than most of us can imagine. We could list a litany of behaviors, character qualities, ideas, and causes to which people are misdirected. **But there is a deeper aspect of love that touches all of us, one we will do well to carefully consider.**

Have you ever been amazed by the single-minded devotion to self-destructive behaviors, or to abusive people, that some people display? Have we been shocked by senseless acts of evil by individuals, or the genocidal obsession of groups? Have we marveled at people's commitments to causes that are obviously false? In our world people line up to be used and abused in the latest ways. We wonder, "Why can't they see?" Because something even bigger than deception is in play. **These people are in love. But, in love with what?**

Remember, we were all born into a nature-sharing covenant with Satan. We were members of his kingdom, and under his authority within his kingdom of darkness. We were taught—thoroughly trained, in fact—to live according to his "ways of the world." For the most part, we followed willingly. If not, vast forces within his kingdom reinforce his ways and coerce any who stray back into line with him—especially if they stray toward God.

We are wired not only to follow God's perfect leadership **but also to follow imperfect and flawed human leaders.** This is a necessity within close human relationships. Mistakes will be made, and we are wired to "hang in there" in the face of many difficulties. This is especially true in Marriage. We hear, **"Love conquers all." This is largely true, but we must consider what must be conquered, and if it truly can be.**

WE ARE ACCUSTOMED TO AN ABUSIVE RELATIONSHIP WITH THE WORLD

Consider a woman in a physically abusive relationship. **She continues to return to her abuser despite every pleading and every reason offered by family and friends.** Her life is miserable. She is in the hands of someone who despises her, who delights in slowly destroying her. Why would anyone return to this situation?

Yet many people return again and again to their abuser. Such a person displays every ounce of commitment, devotion, courage, optimism, and staying power called for by Covenant. She firmly believes her "unconditional love" will change the other. If not, she still believes that this is her best available life. She waits patiently … perhaps at times in hospital emergency rooms. She puts up with any adversity as she discounts the witness of reality and friends. What is missing here? **How can one's virtue and potential become so misdirected?**

Instead of mutual love, **she is seduced and deceived by a false offer of a better together-life**. When one is persuaded that this is truly the best available life, one makes an internal commitment. In doing so, we sign on to the whole package of the other person. One's devotion may then allow grievously dysfunctional and dangerous situations to be simply overlooked. One's inner commitment can overrule all conflicting thoughts—from oneself or others—as eyes are fixed on "what might be, if only …"

No wonder, for even Satan disguises himself as an angel of light.
II Corinthians 11:14

As long as the abused still *believes in* the abuser, he or she will stay the course. People who are truly in love are capable of the most incredible feats of courage, sacrifice, and heroism because of our God-created inner mechanisms.

However, **when commitment is based on deception, behaviors that are appropriate and admirable in a mutual relationship may be a ticket to a morgue, or at the least to a miserable and tortured life.** In this case, such commitment and devotion appear, from the outside, to be totally insane. Yet from the vantage point of the abused, they are doing their very best—as they hang on to a false promise of a better life with everything inside themselves.

In the same way, **the world continues to offer us "reasons for optimism." How many of us believe the hope for our collective future resides in scientific discoveries, technological advances, and education?** Do we still expect "the world system" to right wrongs, provide what is needed, usher in justice, create world peace, and—overall—provide a good and meaningful life for all of us? If it hasn't happened yet—over the last 6,000 years of recorded human history—why hasn't it?

By maintaining our previous commitment to "the world" from whence we came—and **hanging on to our optimism that the world will eventually get things right**—in one sense we display personal integrity. We back up our commitment … and yet that commitment is to our "old life." Since "love never fails," we remain willing to back our commitment in any way necessary. We are willing to overlook the vast inconsistency between promise and performance as we survey our war-torn, degrading, immoral, destructive, and hate-filled world. We wait patiently for things to turn around and head in the right direction—as people have for millennia.

In one sense, it is fortunate that we found a way to hang on to hope in our previous life despite our circumstances. If we had not, we would have been in even more serious trouble. Unfortunately, though, Satan employs our inner commitment, and all the mechanisms God built into us so we can make the most of a Covenant, to sustain our affection toward his world—even after we leave Satan's kingdom. We learned to hang on to our false hope in the worst of circumstances. Now, this groundless optimism is a hard thing to let go of … so that we can fully invest our hope for our future in something entirely different: a totally new life. Or, in Someone who is so different.

How strongly do you believe that the world system will eventually "get things right," and usher in a new era of world peace, prosperity, and happiness by erasing ignorance, disease, poverty, hatred, prejudice, injustice, racism, etc.

100% ______. 75% ______. 50% ______. 25% ______. 10% ______. 0% ______.?

In answer, one might reasonably ask where all of these evils came from in the first place …

Do you believe there is more benefit from strictly following the leadership of God, or from remaining more "open-minded" toward other approaches to life?

____

____

____

CAUGHT BETWEEN TWO LOVES

Despite all evidence to the contrary, somewhere in the depths of our mind and heart we continue to nurture the hope that **we can simply continue the course we walked in our old life and end up with the life we are so sure is out there**, right around the corner—the life we came to believe in, based on a false hope for our future.

If we continue to believe in this life, **we also continue to believe in the being who is the architect of our old life and the world.** If someone (correctly) informs us that this is just a web of lies from Satan, do we believe them—even if this "someone" is God Himself? Or, like the abuse victim we described earlier, do we limp back to our abuser after his latest attack, refusing to acknowledge to ourselves the true nature of the heart we continue to believe in?

Do not love the world or anything in the world. If anyone loves the world, love for the Father is not in them.

I John 2:15

The false hopes of others **may be so glaringly wrong that we are shocked by them.** Yet when our own love is on the line, we may have a bit more difficulty sorting things out. But God calls us to do precisely that. To be willing to fully turn loose of our old life (repent), and fully devote our lives to God, **we must acknowledge that the ruler of the world we continue to believe in is in fact the ultimate betrayer.**

The world under his lordship will not and cannot be transformed into a place of peace, joy, and fulfillment. Why? Satan rebelled against the God of Love; this action alone ensures that true love and satisfaction will never characterize his kingdom. His world can only be headed off a cliff toward eternal judgment by God.

What is our responsibility before God? We are to treat our flesh as if it is our mortal enemy, for it offers only the guidance of our mortal enemy … **guidance that can only kill, steal, and destroy because of who Satan is.**

How much affection do you feel toward the things of the world? Does our discussion impact the way you feel? Take some time to consider what you think and feel about the world, and about its author and lord.

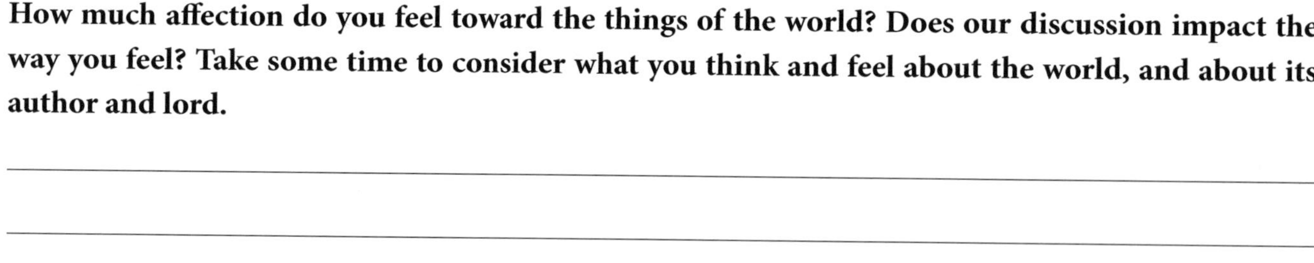

Perhaps we were formerly deceived and believed this enemy's lies. **It is essential to grasp that anything and everything that comes from this source is a lie that is carefully designed to damage and destroy.** Think of toxic waste, or something that is radioactive. This is why God insists that we utterly reject Satan and his ways. This is why the proper term for *turning from God's Lordship to follow Satan* in any way, is sin … a.k.a. rebellion.

Do not love the world nor the things in the world. If anyone loves the world, the love of the Father is not in them. For all that is in the world—the lust of the flesh and the lust of the eyes and the boastful pride of life—is not from the Father, but is from the world. The world is passing away, and also its lusts; but the one who does the will of God lives forever.
I John 2:15-17

ONCE WE RENOUNCE OUR LOVE FOR GOD'S ENEMY, WE ARE FREE TO WHOLEHEARTEDLY LOVE OUR TRUE LORD

We know that we have come to know Him, if we keep His commands. Whoever says, "I know Him," but does not do what He commands, is a liar, and the truth is not in him. But if anyone obeys His word, love for God is truly made complete in them. This is how we know we are in Him: Whoever claims to live in Him must love as Jesus did.
I John 2:3-6

"'You shall worship the Lord your God and serve Him only.'"
Luke 4:8

"THE TRUTH WILL SET YOU FREE …"

God first demands that **we recognize the two sides—first in the celestial battle, and second in the battle within ourselves.** To clear up any confusion, God has provided us with a lengthy written description of His truth, His life, and His love, which we may use to identify any counterfeits offered by His enemy.

It is good to recognize Satan's influence, avoid it, and rid ourselves of its impact when this becomes evident. **But our life in Christ is about far more than not sinning**. Our life in Christ in the New Covenant is about building our new life to its potential.

Our new life is about exploring a new world of obedience, and its beneficial consequences. It is about developing our potential—in our person and our relationships. It is about enjoying our new connection with God and our brothers and sisters in Christ. It is about a new connection with our "new self," and the peace and harmony that result from conforming our beliefs, and thus our inner self, with the new creation that we now are—and with our God. It is about the ultimate gift of Covenant: becoming **an extension of the life of the Creator of All Things.**

Our new life is about exploring every aspect of love—enjoying these through God's love and learning to display these same aspects toward God and others. Then, enjoying these loving relationships, which in turn meet our deepest needs.

Please take a moment and consider what your best possible life might look like.

___

___

___

It just so happens that we must release our death grip on a dying world in order to wholeheartedly approach the task of new-life-building. We will discuss this building process in great detail—both God's plan and our experience as we implement His plan—in coming workbooks. **Here, let us briefly look at the most important aspect of building our new life in Christ.**

EMULATING GOD'S *HESED*

Hesed refers to **God's perfect love** and **Covenant faithfulness.** Both of these, in turn, **proceed from a perfect inner life**. This word represents the totality of God's love. **When God instructs us to "love others as He loves them," is He telling us to reflect all three elements of His love?**

Which of these three is most important? The one from which the other two flow. When we think of "a pure life," we tend to think first of consistently good actions. When we think of Covenant faithfulness, we tend to think about better decision-making. God's Covenant plan has a different focus: our inner life. Perhaps now we can understand why.

What is a pure heart, and why does God want us to have one?

____

____

____

"Blessed are the pure in heart, for they will see God."
MATTHEW 5:8

All who have this hope in Him purify themselves, as He is pure.
I JOHN 3:3

HOW DOES OUR HEART BECOME PURE?

Current teaching suggests that God cleanses us and gives us a pure heart. Here, we have returned to the idea that "God does it all." However, what does I John 3:3 say? **Are we instead to purify ourselves?** In fact, this verse plainly says that we are to engage in a process that results in purity that resembles the purity of Jesus.

In contrast, often in current teaching we are told that we are "pure" because we have been forgiven and cleansed of our sins, and we are "righteous" because God only sees Jesus when He looks at us. While these may be strictly true in terms of our eternal judgement, **these ideas bring us no closer to actually obeying God and loving others.**

If love-as-God-loves, and Covenant faithfulness, proceed forth from a pure heart—and in fact can only come from such a heart—yet our love and faithfulness remain partial and inconsistent, what must we conclude about the "purity" of our heart? **Our hearts still await the purification necessary to produce the life God requires.** How, then, does this purification occur?

Does our discussion to this point suggest an answer?

____

____

____

LOVE FROM A PURE HEART

Our journey toward love and faithfulness makes the most progress when we focus on revising our inner life. Why? Because for love to be wholehearted and for faithfulness to be consistent, we must

devote ourselves to removing those things that pull us in other directions, things that prompt us to disobey, and not-love.

A pure heart is one that simply wants what God wants—one that aligns with His perfect love and faithfulness, one that seeks what is truly best for God, others, and self.

But solid food is for the mature, who because of practice have
their senses trained to distinguish between good and evil.
HEBREWS 5:14

An impure heart yearns for impure, destructive things. Our task is to clear our vision about what is true and what is not … about what is real and what is an illusion … about what is right and what is wrong … and about what is truly beneficial versus what is merely seduction and deception.

God has given us the power—and responsibility—to clear our vision in this way. His Spirit is within us—to reveal our inner life, God's truth, and God's will. God has given us His truth, a book that we may spend the rest of our time on earth digesting, understanding, and applying.

Come near to God and He will come near to you. Wash your hands, you sinners,
and purify your hearts, you double-minded.
JAMES 4:8

Those who live in accordance with the Spirit have their minds set on what the Spirit desires …
the mind governed by the Spirit is life and peace.
ROMANS 8:5, 6

Can you imagine a heart largely devoid of ungodly urges? While we are never fully rid of these things on this earth, this is the task God lays before us. How do you see this task, and what is your plan to accomplish it?

____

____

____

But the goal of our instruction is love from a pure heart,
from a good conscience, and from a sincere faith
I TIMOTHY 1:5 (NASB)

Now that you have purified yourselves by obeying the truth, so that you have a sincere love for each other, love one another deeply, from the heart.
I PETER 1:22

Let us return to the idea of falling in love with God, and consider what goes on within someone as they fall in love. We noted that love in its most powerful form will align our various inner parts, and direct them toward a single imperative: building a together-life with our beloved. **This is the state of our inner being when we have answered all of our questions and put away all of our doubts**. We are now certain that we want to share our life with someone, henceforth and forevermore. **When this state of alignment and focus exists in our mind, heart, and will, what comes forth from us?**

In short, **we will do anything it takes to love our beloved, and to prove to them that our love is genuine.** No one needs to hand us a rule book to show us how to treat the other. Our heart and mind drive us to behave in ways that closely follow God's descriptions of love in Scripture. Everything we do is done to bless and benefit the other.

How would we describe our heart toward the other at this point? **We have purified our heart. We have become wholehearted and single-minded.** At this point people use terms like "true love." This is the inner circuitry of love that God created within us, that is ready to be "turned on" when we are building the most important relationship(s) we will ever have: with our spouse in Covenant, and with who else in Covenant?

What it would be like to have a totally pure heart toward God? What would go on in your mind and heart when you think about God? How enthused would you be to put away anything that interfered with your relationship, and embrace anything that enhanced it? What would you talk about, dream about, plan for, save for, reorder priorities for, and live for?

What you would *not be doing* is longing for, dreaming about, talking about, talking to, or going out with "other gods." We have a strong sense of what true love and wholehearted commitment look like between two people—and the heart behind such things. **God simply wants us to translate this understanding into our relationship with Him.**

A MATTER OF PASSION

What does it mean to be passionate? It means that **our mind, heart, and will are in accord, in a way that moves us to consistent, committed action.** How are love and passion related? Passion is simply the wholehearted outward expression of the alignment and direction of our inner being that is created by wholehearted love. When love is emanating from a pure and undivided heart, everything within us unites in the singleminded pursuit of the object of our affection. But such love may not be fully expressed. **We use the term *passion* to describe such love that is fully unleashed and translated into action.**

This can be contrasted with halfhearted, partial commitment. Of course, minds and hearts can also be fully committed to things that are not good. The term "pure heart" would not apply in a case where one's passions are misdirected toward the wholehearted pursuit of evil.

God asks that our *pure love* translate into *passion*, that is in turn directed toward Him and His purposes. People whose lives are the most transformed, who have experienced the most benefit from following God and implementing His plans, are also the most passionate about Him. The more one resembles Christ, the more passionate one will be about Him.

Are you passionate about your God and your relationship with Him? Are you in love with your Lord and Savior? Are you all about God and His Kingdom? Is everything within you aligned with God's heart and desire? If not, would you like this to be true? Do you believe this could be your life? If so, how? Outline your personal plan to fall more deeply in love with your Lord, and remove anything that stands in your way.

* * * * * * *

THE SUM OF GOD'S MESSAGE TO US ABOUT LOVING AS HE DOES

- We must recognize the spiritual battleground we inhabit.
- We must clearly understand the nature and agenda of the two sides in this war.
- We must recognize the nature of the relationship we have entered with God:

- The changes that occurred within us and between us as we entered Covenant;
- The consequences of these changes, and how these are to guide our new life.

- We must recognize the difference between our old life and our new life—the author of each plan for living, and the outcome of each way of life.
- In order to fulfill God's plan, and the imperatives of Covenant—consistent love-in-action and unremitting faithfulness—we must rid ourselves of the guidance of God's enemy and our affection for his guidance, and devote ourselves solely to God and His Lordship.
- This is essential if we are to accomplish God's plan of transformation—from our old self and old life to our new self, and live an entirely new life.
- This, in turn, requires that we understand:

  A) that we are already transformed in the core of our being so that this *new life* authentically expresses "who we are";

  B) that we understand our new life to be "our life" as an extension of the life of God. "My life" no longer exists within Covenant;

  C) that our best possible life—the most rewarding, fulfilling, and blessed—is found by obeying God and carefully carrying out His plan for our life, which in turn requires that we be transformed by the renewing of our mind.

- This alteration of our belief system shifts the foundation of our decision-making and the fabric of our being from the lies of God's enemy to the Truth of God.
- This in turn shifts our mind, heart, and will into alignment with the Life of God. This shifts the fabric of our being—our character, guidance system for living, and self-image—into alignment with the Life of God.
- At the same time, this progressively dismantles our "flesh"—the aspects of our lives that oppose the work of God in our lives.
- All of this now allows us to function in alignment with what is true, real, right, and beneficial. We recognize—and experience—the benefit of God's Truth and His ways.
- Therefore, our desire for Him and His ways naturally grows into *a passion for the things of God.*
- As the thoughts and ways of Satan are subtracted from our hearts, our hearts become pure. That is, our hearts become purely devoted to the things of God.
- Love is a force that aligns everything within us toward a single purpose: to build a together-life with the object of our love. So, inasmuch as God's life is within us, our "true self" now aligns with God's life. His life and resources are freely available to us according to our faithfulness. Now we can express

our love for God and those in His body using not only our resources, but the resources and power of the Living God. This is the way God wants us to build His Kingdom here on earth, and for all of eternity.

- As with our Lord's *hesed*, this is how our pure heart is to be expressed—through purely beneficial actions and unremitting faithfulness within our Covenant; and also expressed to those outside His Kingdom, who desperately need to experience the presence of a human life that expresses the love of the God they so desperately need to know. This is God's heart toward those in our lost and dying world.

THE BEST LIFE WE CAN LIVE IS …

What is the best life you or I could possibly live? The answer you get depends on who you ask. A huge array of ideas are being field-tested at this moment, and have been throughout human history. Our undying optimism aside, as we look around, how well are these ideas working? Is our world characterized by love, joy, peace, contentment, and gratitude? If not now, when has it ever been? Instead, what does characterize our world?

I used to put "how to live" ideas into three categories: 1) the things of God; 2) the things that are frankly evil—that obviously come from Satan; and 3) the vast array of ideas that we term "human diversity"—which arise from attempts by individuals and cultures to solve the problems of life. But this view has shifted over the decades as I watch various ways of life play out, even in this life. There are actually only two categories: "the things of God" and "other." Why am I so sure of this?

"The devil…was a murderer from the beginning, not holding to the truth, for there is no truth in him. When he lies, he speaks his native language, for he is a liar and the father of lies."
John 8:44

Consider the distinction between "the things of God" and "other." Why is there a sharp and clear line between these two? We must consider what "truth" is, and the alternative to truth. Truth is a correct statement of what is happening, what did happen, and what is going to happen. Anything other than truth is not true. These ideas are mistaken and mislead us. We must also consider the authors of these ideas, who are on each side of a vast chasm. One is the God of all truth. The other is the "father of lies." Truth is an accurate rendering of what is actually true, right, real, and beneficial. **What are we hearing, then, when we hear something different?**

Ideas, beliefs, and choices have real consequences, which are determined by the moral universe God created for us to inhabit. What we think, hope, or believe will happen in response to our choices does not determine outcomes. So, if we are misled about what is real, or right, or beneficial, and we act accordingly, what are we building? Far more than we realize, each of us is assembling a group of consequences, viewpoints, assumptions, values, goals, preferences, agendas, strategies, along with a character, guidance system, and self-image, which are based—at least in part—on misinformation. Keep in mind that this is about more than simply not seeing things clearly, or not being "entirely right" about something. This conversation is about the accumulation of millennia of misinformation that has been fed to the human race, which is carefully designed to entice us to depart from our Creator.

Thanks to the way our minds work, once we are persuaded to embrace these ideas as "our truth," we firmly believe we have arrived at the best approach to life … given our circumstances.

Yet, in the midst of the life we create for ourselves, **we often find ourselves missing something of vital importance.** We experience a lack of love. We do not feel the love that we desire, and need. We do not know how to love. We have tried to substitute everything the world has offered to make up for this lack … but this never works. **There truly is no substitute for love.**

And over all these virtues put on love, which binds them all together in perfect unity.
COLOSSIANS 3:14

The most important question we will ever answer is this:

"Who do you say that I am?"
MARK 8:29

We may verbally identify Jesus correctly as God-come-in-the-flesh, and as our Savior and Lord. If Jesus is truly God, the Creator, the Author of life, truth, and love, then we would logically regard His life (as the Word who became flesh—John 1:1-4, 14) and His Word as the definition of truth … period. If this is true, and **we have made Him our Lord, then logically His Word should rule in our lives, and overrule any and every competing idea.**

"Why do you call me 'Lord, Lord,' and do not do what I say?"
LUKE 6:46

Do we truly grasp the absurdity of recognizing who Jesus is, then saying that we believe Him and believe in Him (which we must if we are to enter the New Covenant with Him), then publicly proclaiming that He is our Lord and Savior (which we do through baptism) … **then, basing our decisions on a competing and conflicting set of ideas that come from a being in rebellion against the God we say we love and proclaim to be our Lord?** We must somehow believe that God is okay with this response, and that some other course of action is actually better for us than the directives of God.

From a purely practical standpoint, what is going to build our best life? If we understand what is really true about self, God, life, and relationships; if we can understand what is real—versus what is imaginary; if we can understand what is right—versus what is wrong morally in a sense that extends far beyond sexuality; and if we can understand what is truly beneficial—versus false sales pitches for useless and destructive things ... then we would live our best life. If we then direct our lives accordingly, would this not produce a better life than one we could build following any other guidance?

Do we really want a life that is directed toward best results; or do we want a life that is intentionally misdirected away from God, toward destruction? The problem with deception is that, despite the obvious negative results of its guidance, we are wired to press through adversity—even self-imposed adversity—ever more sure that we are on the right path. We have decided for ourselves that the promised benefits of our choices will one day shower down upon us ... not realizing that all of this merely represents the false promises of our abusive "lover."

"What profit will a person have if he gains the whole world, but destroys himself or is lost?"
LUKE 9:25 (ISV)

If we are seeking our best life, what about love—that essential element that nourishes our souls in a way that nothing else can? The enemy promises love, but offers the fleeting sensations of meaningless sexual activity, or a pile of money to gaze upon, or the impersonal adulation of fame ... or simply searing loneliness, as we burn the bridges to those around us in our pursuit of ... something that will never satisfy.

So, if we seek to build a life characterized by love—or a church body, or the whole Body of Christ on this earth—what must be done? To fully appreciate God's instructions, we must realize that **everything that His enemy has ever said, done, or falsely offered is designed to lead us to not-love other people, and to disobey God ... period.**

Everything God has ever said, done, or offered **is designed to produce love, faithfulness, and blessing. All of this is ultimately intended to allow us to emulate the life of Christ in every way that our finiteness allows.** God did everything necessary within us that we could not do, and provided every needed resource through the New Covenant so we can fulfill His assignment to build our new life.

What does God say about building our best life?

So I tell you this, and insist on it in the Lord, that you must no longer live as the Gentiles do, in the futility of their thinking. They are darkened in their understanding and separated from the life of God because of the ignorance that is in them due to the hardening of their hearts. Having lost all sensitivity, they have given themselves over to sensuality so as to indulge in every kind of impurity, and they are full of greed. That, however, is not the way of life you learned when you heard about Christ and were taught in him in accordance with the truth that is in Jesus. You were taught, with respect to your former way of life, to put off your old self, which is being corrupted by its deceitful desires; to be made new in the attitude of your minds; and to put on the new self, created to be like God in true righteousness and holiness.

EPHESIANS 4:17-24

Wash your hands, you sinners, and purify your hearts, you double-minded.
James 4:8

We demolish arguments and every pretension that sets itself up against the knowledge of God, and we take captive every thought to make it obedient to Christ.
2 Corinthians 10:5

Sadly, **many voices within the Christian community say that God's Word is not an infallible source of truth.** These people must therefore replace the real "bottom line" source of truth with something else. Who do you think rushes in to fill this void? Those who deny the authority of the Scriptures often go on to declare as "truth" the agenda and deceptions of God's enemy about what is real, true, right, and good.

Even for those who say—in theory—that God's Word is the ultimate source of truth, **there is little clarity about the importance of bringing our life into line with God's life**. What happens next? Inevitably, people continue much of their old life. This is the "one foot in the Kingdom of God, but the other foot firmly planted somewhere else" plan. What does God say about those in His Kingdom who continue to embrace their old lies and lives?

What do righteousness and wickedness have in common?
Or what fellowship can light have with darkness?

2 CORINTHIANS 6:14

They exchanged the truth of God for a lie, and worshipped
and served created things, rather than the Creator.

ROMANS 1:25

Woe to those who call evil good and good evil, who turn darkness to light,
and light to darkness, who replace bitter with sweet, and sweet with bitter.

ISAIAH 5:20 (BSB)

Let no one deceive you with empty words, for because of such things God's wrath comes on those who are disobedient. Therefore do not be partners with them.

EPHESIANS 5:6-7

If we deliberately keep on sinning after we have received the knowledge of the truth, no sacrifice for sins is left, but only a fearful expectation of judgement and of raging fire that will consume the enemies of God. Anyone who rejected the law of Moses died without mercy on the testimony of two or three witnesses. How much more severely do you think someone deserves to be punished who has trampled the Son of God underfoot, who has treated as an unholy thing the blood of the Covenant that sanctified them, and who has insulted the Spirit of grace? For we know him who said, "it is mine to avenge; I will repay," and again, "the Lord will judge his people." It is a dreadful thing to fall into the hands of the living God.

HEBREWS 10:26-31

No one who lives in Him keeps on sinning. No one who keeps on sinning has either seen Him or known Him…The one who does what is sinful is of the devil, because the devil has been sinning from the beginning. The reason the Son of God appeared was to destroy the devil's work.

I JOHN 3:6,8

EACH OF US IS LEFT WITH ONE KEY QUESTION TO ANSWER

If we could do, and be, and become all that God instructs, and live the life He desires for us, would this truly be our best possible life? What do you think, and why?

____

____

____

____

____

____

KNOWING AND CARRYING OUT GOD'S PLAN

Thus, if our lives are to change in such ways, we need a plan to move from where we are to where we want to be. We briefly outlined this plan … on paper. This is a necessary first step.

But this is not the same as walking through all of this in reality. We can watch someone scale a steep mountain. This is not the same as developing the skills needed to climb this same rock face. Then, to use every bit of training, strength, understanding, and willpower that is necessary to move from the bottom of the mountain to its top—this is another matter entirely. We must overcome the obstacles: gravity, wind, and limited visibility. Along the way, we must make correct decisions with, literally, every step, and prevail in our internal struggle, as we entrust our life to a single handhold time after time. We may have the ability, but we must overcome many things within ourselves to succeed in the end.

Volume Two: GOD'S PLAN / OUR FAITHFULNESS covers the necessary training process by which we are actually equipped to do, be, and become what God desires.

Volume Three: OUR JOURNEY leads us through the challenges and experiences we will encounter. We must learn how to savor the delight of our journey with our Lord, as we overcome in His Name and build the life He intends for us.

OTHER BOOKS IN THE COVENANT SERIES

MARK JOHNSON, MD and HOLLEY JOHNSON, MS, RDH

The best defense of Biblical Marriage in our generation!

...and the best case for faithfulness, the foundation for Revival!

WHAT IS A COVENANT? Rather than a CONTRACT (the current teaching), COVENANT is entered via ***an exchange of identity*** with another. The two are joined by ***a bond of identity,*** and ***the identity of each is altered***—the "one flesh" bond of Marriage, or a new creature indwelled by the Holy Spirit. Covenant is not just a tie that binds. Inherent **in the nature and structure of Covenant is a plan—that is all about love, and all about faithfulness.** We are told to love; taught God's definition of love; offered many new motivations to love; and transformed—so that we become able to love deeply and consistently across the spectrum of life and relationship...if we follow God's plan.

THE COVENANT OF MARRIAGE Join us as we examine ***God's Covenant plan for Marriage.*** First, the nature of Marriage—the **exchange of identity** as we enter it and **the bond that is formed.** Then, the implications of the ***transformation*** that occurs as we wed. God's intends that we **shift our way of life**—*our decisions, values, and priorities*—into accord with the reality of our nature and our relationship. We examine how this is done and the quality of relationship this shift produces. In addition to creating the best relationship, this approach produces the best version of us. Which, in turn, allows us to build the best possible life.

THE NEW COVENANT Once in Covenant with God, *who have we become, and what are we supposed to do?* The answers are found in the nature, structure, and function of a Covenant. We are ***new beings*** in a ***new bond with God, indwelled by His Spirit.*** Love and obedience are the native language of this new being, and the commands of our Lord But this authentic life is opposed by a guidance system we acquired from *the world.* By *transforming our mind,* this guidance system can change. We *put off* the external life produced by our old guidance system, and *put on* an external life that authentically expresses the being we have become—we **live up to** what **we have already attained.** God's foremost commands are to love—Him and others. His Covenant plan is designed to produce ***faithful people***, capable of loving Him and others across the spectrum of human experience...***if we follow God's plan.***

ABOUT THE AUTHORS

Dr. Johnson has focused on personal spiritual growth, mentoring, and teaching for over forty years. Following his introduction to the historic understanding of Covenant in a Kay Arthur Bible study in 1983, his efforts integrated around *the nature of His relationship* with God, and his marriage. He terms this understanding, "the most important single thing I have ever learned in my life before God." Mark and Holley not only built spiritual lives upon this foundation, but also their marriage—field-testing these concepts and approaches while raising seven children and building a multifaceted life together. The two built a medical practice which draws patients from across the nation and many foreign countries. Dr. Johnson is a teacher, mentor, and researcher in his specialty. Mark and Holley want to share the things they have found most important in life—things they are convinced represent *the very heart of God's plan for each of us.* They live in the Nashville, Tennessee area.